THE

TAO

OF
HEALTH AND
LONGEVITY

THE

TAO

OF
HEALTH AND
LONGEVITY

REVISED AND EXPANDED EDITION/ILLUSTRATED

Da Liu

PARAGON HOUSE

NEW YORK

First Paragon House edition, 1991

Published in the United States by

Paragon House Publishers
90 Fifth Avenue
New York, N.Y. 10011

Library of Congress Cataloging-in-Publishing data
Da, Liu.
    The Tao of health and longevity / by Da Liu. — New and expanded ed., 1st Paragon Houses ed.
        p.   cm.
    Includes index.
    ISBN 1-55778-436-1 : $9.95 (pbk.)
    1. Hygiene, Taoist. 2. Health. 3. T'ai chi ch'üan.
4. Longevity.   I. Title.
RA776.5.D3   1990
613.7—dc20

90-14163
CIP

To order an instructional videotape containing the complete movements of T'ai Chi Ch'uan found in this book send a check for $70.00 to the T'ai Chi Society of New York, 520 West 110th Street, Apartment 7A, New York, NY 10025

ACKNOWLEDGMENTS

I would like to thank the following for their help in completing this manuscript: Dr. Jean MacRae Landon, Dr. Samuel Johnson, Rosemary Birardi, Paul Knopf, Sharon Wheeler Hadley, Ewen Gillies, T. C. Chang, Steven Berko, Noa Nothman, S. P. Wang, Reggie Jackson, Duncan Cooper, Ortega Luise, Tracy Cochran.

September, 1990
Da Liu

CONTENTS

vi   Contents

5

HOW TO PERFORM THE T'AI CHI CH'UAN
FORM   *52*

6

ADDITIONAL EXERCISE TECHNIQUES OF
THE TAOIST TRADITION   *108*

A Simple Standing Form
Swinging Arms
Eight Pieces of Treasure
Exercises That Can Be Done in Bed
Seated Breathing
Standing Exercise
Sitting Meditation

7

HEALTH IN DAILY LIFE   *130*

Food
Clothing
Shelter
Daily Activity

8

SELF-TREATMENT: THE METHODS OF
MASSAGE AND ACUPRESSURE   *146*

Massage
Acupressure
Moxa and Fire Treatment

9

THE PREVENTION AND TREATMENT OF THE MAJOR DISEASES THROUGH EXERCISE AND MEDITATION

10

FOOD AS MEDICINE

11

CHINESE HEALTH FOOD

12

THE RELATIONSHIP BETWEEN MAN AND WOMAN

13

PEACE OF MIND

PREFACE TO THE PARAGON HOUSE EDITION

Health and longevity are the central principles of Taoism. In 2697 B.C. Hwang Ti, the Yellow Emperor, asked the great sage, Kwang Cheng Tze, "How should I rule my body, in order that it may continue for a long time?" Kwang Cheng Tze replied:

> There is nothing to be seen, nothing to be heard. Hold your spirit in stillness; your body becomes correct (healthy). . . . You must be still. You must be pure, not subjecting your body to toil, not agitating your vital force . . . then you may live for long. . . . I maintain the (original) unity (of these elements), and dwell in the harmony of them. In this way I have cultivated myself for one thousand and two hundred years, and my bodily form has undergone no decay.[1]

Later Hwang Ti wrote his important opus, *Nei Ching*, (*Classic of Inner Medicine*), translated by Ilza Veith, which details many ways to prevent and cure disease. This volume is an essential resource for anyone who wishes to study Chinese techniques and is still used as a textbook by many Chinese medical doctors. I will elaborate on some of the principles of this book in the Introduction. Basically, Hwang Ti said that the good doctor should prevent sickness rather than cure disease. Prevention has continued to be a key principle for Eastern physicians, and today we are particularly concerned with the prevention of cancer and cardiovascular disease.

Various forms of cancer have caused death and disease the world over. The threat of this catastrophic illness often seems as fearful as nuclear proliferation. Every day it seems we are made aware of a new carcinogen, whether chemical, physical, or psychological. In addition to the discussion of cancer-preventing foods in Chapter 9, I have added more material specifically related to cancer. It is reassuring to find that ancient beliefs about the prevention and treatment of cancer are being rediscovered and affirmed by modern medical science. In this edition I will review the relationships between the old and the new and present positive suggestions for the prevention—even the cure—of cancer.

Although cancer is a visible and frightening threat to our health and longevity, heart disease is still the number one killer and source of disability in the United States. The abundance of media coverage on cardiovascular disease, heart attacks, atherosclerosis, and strokes attests to growing public concern. It has been shown that the major risk factors for heart disease are hypertension, poor nutrition, lack of exercise, stress, and smoking. The principles covered in this book, and the regimen of exercise, nutrition, and meditation provided (if faithfully followed) can mitigate all of these risk factors, except possibly the last.

For many years practitioners of Western medicine were skeptical about the ancients' advice on the prevention and cure of disease. Then Asian experts with training in Western science began to proclaim the values of the traditional use of herbs and point to the health benefits of a particular life-style. During his sixty years of medical practice, much of it as a cancer specialist, Dr. William Chao made important discoveries about the prevention and cure of cancer. His findings are contained in his book, *Chinese Cancer*

Therapy, which will be discussed in the chapter on the major diseases. Also, Michio Kushi, a Japanese expert, has written about the use of food and exercise, including T'ai Chi Ch'uan, yoga, and meditation, to deal with cancer. His methods are described in his book, *The Cancer Prevention Diet*.[2] His principles are similar to mine, which I have explained in several of my books.

Scientific research now supports many of the old beliefs about health and longevity. For example, the idea of moderate exercise to help prevent cancer and other serious ailments is no longer solely an Asian one. A recent New York *Times* article reported on a major study on exercise and fitness. The article states, "The largest study measuring fitness ever carried out suggests that even modest amounts of exercise can substantially reduce a person's chance of dying of heart disease, cancer, or other causes."[3] The most striking finding was that the biggest health gain came not from seeking the fitness achieved by dedicated athletes, but from just getting out of the most sedentary category. "This is a hopeful message, an important message for the American people to understand,"[4] said Dr. Carl Casperson of the Centers for Disease Control in Atlanta.

As for nutrition, its importance in the prevention and treatment of disease is now amply supported. A recent publication[5] lists 513 references in the scientific literature on dietary factors related to health. The research now being done by Dr. Dean Ornish at the Preventive Medicine Research Institute at Sausalito, California, goes beyond exercise and nutrition and includes meditation as an essential element in its program for the treatment of heart disease patients. The findings of Dr. Ornish's study, described in a recent New York *Times* article,[4] are especially relevant to the principles I describe in the following chapters. Dr. Ornish sees meditation as a way of dealing with stress: "The stress-control component is often ignored, but several studies show stress plays a major role in the development of atherosclerosis."

This new edition of my book should prove especially useful in this time of increasing stress. Living in industrial cities, people are subjected to overcrowding, high noise levels, transportation delays, and constant pressure to speed up their lives. They—or their acquaintances—become crime victims. Society's unsolved problems weigh on them when they see the homeless in the streets. Job-related stress is endemic. Even increased knowledge can sometimes add to stress, for as people become aware of the need for proper nutrition and exercise, they worry about the interference presented by their busy schedules.

Among my students I find some who are overstimulated by their many activities; they find no time to relax and clear their minds. Sometimes they are confused by the conflicting values they encounter. They want and need a health plan that offers help with exercise and nutrition and, above all, inner peace. My own observations and experience during the last ten years, and correspondence from readers, have made it clear to me that a new, revised edition of my book is needed.

NOTES

1. James Legge, *Texts of Taoism* Part 1 (New York: Dover Publications). 1962, pp. 298–99.

2. Michio Kushi, *The Cancer Prevention Diet* (New York: St. Martin's Press) 1983.

3. Philip J. Hilts, "Exercise and Longevity: A Little Goes a Long Way," The New York *Times*, November 3, 1989.

4. Ibid.

5. Mark F. McCarthy, *Health Benefits of Supplemental Nutrition*, 2nd ed. (Nutriguard Research, 1988).

6. Daniel Coleman, "Life-Style Shift Can Unclog Ailing Arteries, Study Finds," The New York *Times*, November 14, 1989.

PREFACE

According to a saying well known in China, when people are young, they wish to be heroes and patriotic revolutionaries. When they are middle-aged, they wish to be scholarly eccentrics. When they are old, they wish to become hermits, withdraw from the world, and lead a peaceful life. Reflecting on my own experience, I find that my life fits this general pattern rather well.

When I was young, I incessantly read stories about great warriors and adventurers and enthusiastically learned many kinds of strenuous martial arts such as Shao Lin (similar to what Westerners call karate). When not studying at school, I could often be found practicing these forms of violence in the temple of my ancestral clan, punching walls, kicking trees, and so on.

Later, as a college student, I began to learn the far more gentle discipline of T'ai Chi Ch'uan. Although this discipline also involved a highly refined method of self-defense, I was much more intrigued by its philosophical aspects, the way it incorporated the ancient wisdom of Taoism. In fact, I abandoned the practice of the strenuous martial arts at this time and devoted most of my energy to the careful study of the ancient philosophical classics: the *I Ching*, the works of Lao Tzu, Chuang Tzu, and others.

Later on, after the war interrupted my scholarly career, I came to the United States, where I worked for the United Nations. Before long, I began to teach T'ai Chi Ch'uan classes at the United Nations, the China Institute, and the YWCA. At that time, T'ai Chi was virtually unknown in this country, and the classes attracted considerable attention from the media. During the late 1950's and early 1960's, I made several television appearances, and my story, together with information about the T'ai Chi exercises, appeared in many newspapers and magazines, including the New York *Herald-Tribune, Newsweek, Vogue, Mademoiselle, McCall's,* and even *Children's Day.* Most people connected with these publications were especially interested in the self-defense aspects of T'ai Chi and seemed to want spectacular martial arts demonstrations. A few people, however, particularly one of my students who was a physical therapist, suggested that I could do a lot more good by emphasizing the health aspects of the exercises.

By the time I published my first book on the subject, in 1972, *T'ai Chi Ch'uan and I Ching,*[1] I entirely agreed with this point of view. The book was mainly philosophical and health oriented and mentioned techniques of self-defense only briefly. After it was published, however, I began to think about how to make the information about the exercises readily available to those people who would be most likely to benefit from it. For several years, people who had read about me in magazines had been impressed with the fact that the practice of T'ai Chi is so effortless and gentle that it is an ideal form of exercise for anyone who cannot or does not want to practice more strenuous methods of physical fitness. Indeed, some who had seen the articles in women's magazines suggested that I write a book on T'ai Chi for women. Others, who were particularly struck by the fact that the exercises could be successfully learned and practiced even by people of very advanced age, suggested that I address myself especially to the elderly.

The more I thought about it, however, the more clearly I saw that T'ai Chi Ch'uan should not be presented so as to appear especially valuable to one particular group of people, for the remarkable truth about T'ai Chi is that it has a universal value as a health practice unmatched by any other form of exercise. Over the many years that I have been teaching these exercises, I have had very young and very old students, men as well as women, of many different religions and occupations, and have seen the benefits enjoyed by all who had the patience and perseverance to learn them and practice them regularly.

Among my students have been several actors, dancers, musicians, and other performing artists who have found their arts greatly advanced by the improved balance, coordination, and relaxation they developed through T'ai Chi. Other students were sick, disabled, or dependent on drugs when they began to learn and found the practice of T'ai Chi an invaluable aid in regaining good health. The exact nature of the health benefits one can expect from the practice is to some extent dependent on one's health situation and point of view. Of course there are many different situations and points of view, but the important thing is that everyone who makes these exercises part of his or her life discovers a unique value in them.

The universal value of T'ai Chi comes from the fact that, though it has its roots in the ancient Chinese classics, it incorporates in a practical way a profoundly wise understanding of health and longevity that is almost completely applicable in modern society. Most of the forms of sport and exercise widely practiced in both the East and West today are highly competitive and emphasize strength and quick reflexes. Excellence in these activities is limited to the young, especially those who undergo strenuous training designed to increase their strength and stamina. Those who cannot compete successfully tend to be relegated to the role of spectators. As a result, many people do not become involved with exercise in a way that is good for their health.

At the same time, many people today tend to think of health only in terms of curing sickness, and longevity only in terms of avoiding fatal diseases. But while it is true that by discovering ways of curing and preventing infectious diseases, medical science has greatly increased the longevity of the average person, it is also becoming recognized that mere survival into old age is not enough. Many elderly people cannot enjoy their retirement years and are very unhappy because of health problems and deterioration of physical capabilities.

What T'ai Chi Ch'uan offers as an alternative is a much broader concept of health and longevity, according to which an organism flourishes only if it is properly nourished and cared for throughout its life cycle. In order for a tree to bear good fruit, it must be watered and cultivated from the time it is a tiny sprout, through its branching, leaf-growing, and flowering stages. Strength is of some importance to a tree, so that it will not be broken by the wind, but it is only one factor in good health. It is likewise for people. The exercises and other health practices described in this book are techniques that can be applied by anyone on a regular basis. They will not only greatly increase muscular strength but will also promote growth, help prevent physical deterioration, and lead to good health and a happy old age.

T'ai Chi Ch'uan, however, is more than a mere technique, for it has deep spiritual aspects. It is very important to emphasize that the achievement of health and longevity cannot be attained simply by a mechanical application of techniques.

I recently read of the death of General Yang Sen, a

former military commander in China who was famous in Taiwan as an advocate of physical fitness and longevity.[2] In the 1920's, he came to know the remarkable Taoist master Li Ch'ing Yuen, who lived to be 250 years old. He arranged to photograph Master Li and later wrote a book about him that received wide publicity. Yang Sen believed that this case of unusual longevity was amazing because it was accomplished without scientific understanding on the part of Li Ch'ing Yuen; he also felt that by practicing the kind of exercise Master Li had used, which was similar to T'ai Chi Ch'uan, and in addition taking advantage of modern scientific knowledge related to human health, it would not be difficult to live a healthy life to a very great age. He was fond of demonstrating his own good health and vigor, often appearing in public to perform prodigious athletic feats and to make speeches about longevity and physical fitness. The New York *Times* obituary reported that, on his ninety-sixth birthday, he went on a long hike in the mountains followed by more than 10,000 people. A Nationalist Chinese publication, *New Martial Hero* magazine, recently told of a speech he gave in which he promised to make a trip around the world after his 100th birthday to publicize further his longevity techniques. Many people were thus surprised and disappointed when he died of lung cancer, while still in his nineties.

In the 1930's, while he was commander of the Chinese forces during the war against the Japanese, I came to know Yang Sen personally, and since that time I have kept informed about his activities and writings. I believe that his methods of health and longevity were quite good and that his efforts to make them more widely known were valuable. I too was surprised by the news of his death. On further reflection, however, I came to feel that a lesson can be learned from his untimely death as well as from his long and healthy life. Of course, cancer is a complex, poorly understood disease. One should be careful about speculating concerning its causes, which no doubt involve a number of chemical, physiological, and perhaps emotional factors. Nevertheless, I cannot help observing that Yang Sen's routine of public exposure and self-demonstration must have been rather exciting and, as a result, a significant drain on his energy. To engage in such activities is far away from the ideal of nonaction and withdrawal from the world that the ancient Taoist classics tell us is the key to peace of mind.

The New York *Times* has also reported recently on a number of people whose longevity far exceeds that of Yang Sen. Nearly 20,000 centenarians live in rural areas in the Soviet Union; some of them are over 150 years old. In America, the oldest citizen, according to the Social Security Administration, is Charlie Smith, who is 135.[3] These exceptionally long-lived people have invariably lived humble lives, doing hard physical work, often outdoors, from early youth until well into old age. Their diet is very simple, and their social lives mainly involve their extended families, which revere and respect them. Although these people are no doubt ignorant of the techniques of health and longevity practiced by Yang Sen, their active yet uncomplicated lives realize the spiritual ideal of the Taoist classics. Shirali Mislimov, a 170-year-old gardener in the Soviet Azerbaijan region, puts it as follows: "I am never in a hurry. So don't be in a hurry to live, this is the main thing. Then one must observe a physical daily regimen, of course. I have been doing physical work for 150 years."[4]

Over the years, I have watched many friends grow old. Some who did not practice exercises or other longevity techniques still lived long and happily because they were humble and quietly at peace with themselves. Others died prematurely even though they practiced health exercises because they could not control their emotions; they became angry or very depressed as a result of losing family members, jobs, or money. I have become convinced that the Taoist concept of avoiding strong emotions and excitement is really important for a successful old age. Thus I have included in the book an introduction to Taoist philosophy, which I hope will give the reader some understanding of how to achieve its ideal of inner peace and quiet. It is my wish that by taking this philosophy to heart as well as practicing the exercises I describe, using the information about self-treatment, and avoiding bad habits and carelessness that cause unnecessary diseases, the reader will enjoy a rich reward in his or her old age.

NOTES

1. (New York: Harper and Row, 1972).
2. New York *Times*, May 17, 1977.
3. New York *Times*, July 20, 1977.
4. New York *Times*, September 9, 1977, p. 4A.

CHAPTER 1:

INTRODUCTION

The final quarter of the twentieth century is witnessing the emergence of longevity as an important value. There can be little doubt that it is an idea whose time has come. Only a short time ago, most people throughout the world died before they were fifty, and the prospect of living to old age was realized only by a few exceptional individuals. In the past few decades, however, there has been vast improvement in the control of infectious and contagious diseases, the reduction of infant and maternal death rates, and the quality of public health and sanitation. As a result, the percentage of the population surviving to advanced age has steadily increased, to the point where the elderly, at least in the developed countries, constitute a substantial minority group in society. In the United States, the average life expectancy at birth has increased to more than 70 years for men and 72 for women. It is even higher in some countries in Europe. Projections of current trends indicate that in every region of the world, the rate of increase of the 65 and over age group during the decade from 1970 to 1980 will be greater than that of any other age group, and also greater than that of the world's population as a whole.

This phenomenon of increased longevity has affected society in a variety of ways. Of course, it is a great benefit for large numbers of people to experience full maturity of years, to rest after completing their lifelong work, and to see the development of their children and grandchildren. In addition, the experience and wisdom of elderly people represents a significant resource, which, if properly organized, can be of benefit to the rest of society as well. On the other hand, increasingly widespread longevity has led to problems and difficulties that are only beginning to be fully appreciated and that sometimes seem to outweigh the benefit resulting from it. Unfortunately, the reality of old age for many people is an unhappy one, in which they may suffer losses of numerous kinds: loss of effectiveness of perception such as vision and hearing, loss of energy, loss of a conventionally attractive appearance, loss of income, loss of the challenge and responsibility of the work role, loss of spouse and friends. In the face of these losses and the resulting stress and anxiety, it is not surprising that many old people soon also lose their self-respect, grow sick and become invalids, and fail to enjoy any of the benefits of increased longevity.

The current attempts to solve these problems and obtain the benefits of longevity are of two main types: (1) scientific research aimed at improving understanding of the biological and sociological aspects of aging; and (2) policies and programs of various governmental and social institutions aimed at improving the quality of life for the aged. The various processes involved in aging are indeed becoming more clearly identified and better understood through research work in gerontology, which is now being done by groups of scientists at various places throughout the world. But the most fundamental question of what causes living organisms to age, and their vital systems to wear out and deteriorate, is very difficult to answer in chemical and biological terms. It is fair to say that science is far from any type of knowledge that could be generally applied to delay significantly or prevent the deterioration of aging.

Efforts by government and other institutions to improve the quality of life for the elderly have been increasing at all levels. At the international level, the General Assembly of the United Nations has resolved to investigate the conditions and needs of the elderly and to develop guidelines for national policies and international action. In response to this, a meeting of experts on aging has been held at United Nations headquarters, and the Secretary General prepared a report.[1] In the United States, the elderly have become a powerful political force, and there are a variety of programs designed to benefit them. Current legislation in Congress that would end mandatory retirement at sixty-five for civil service workers appears likely to pass, and the mandatory retirement policy is also being abolished by many private businesses. Similar developments are occurring elsewhere in the world, in the Soviet Union, for example, which has a large elderly population. Recent articles in *Pravda* have suggested that the government is reconsidering its policy on retirement, which presently allows men to retire at sixty and women at fifty-five, in the light of evidence that regular participation in useful work is essential to health and happiness in old age.[2] Increasingly, local governments are administering a variety of programs to assist the elderly in fulfilling their needs for health care, safety, transportation, rent control, and other essentials of life.

All of these efforts are certainly good and should continue to increase in order to make this assistance more widely available. But at the same time, it should be recognized that the response of the institutions of society is necessarily limited and cannot ultimately supply good health and well-being to the people.

Moreover, such response is also limited in that it treats the problem of aging only insofar as it affects those who have already attained old age. Actually, the ability of a person to enjoy good health and happiness in old age is quite dependent on his or her activities earlier in life.

The limitations of these ways of approaching the problems of longevity suggest that new ideas are needed. It would be particularly valuable if an approach could be developed that would be based on the recognition that longevity is a value not just for old people but for all people and that would provide information which could be applied by all people regardless of age or health condition to take action on their own toward the attainment of good health and happy longevity. It is my conviction that such an approach exists and can be found in the traditional wisdom of China. Although not widely known in the West at present, it could greatly improve the prospects for good health throughout life into longevity of people everywhere when it becomes more generally known.

In China, the aims of good health and greater longevity have been approached systematically since early antiquity, when several kinds of technique were developed for the purpose of attaining immortality. The practice of these techniques can be traced back to Hwang Ti, the so-called Yellow Emperor, who ruled China for a century during the third millennium B.C. His practices included T'u Na, a breathing exercise, and a kind of gentle calisthenics called Tao Yin, which means "leading and guiding." These methods were forerunners of the techniques of meditation and exercise practiced today and described in this book. In addition, he engaged in a number of sexual practices with his many wives that he believed would enable him to be immortal. These he described in a series of discussions with a woman named Su Nu, who was perhaps his concubine. The record of their discussions later came to be known as the *Su Nu Ching*.[3] Hwang Ti also discussed several medical topics, including methods of curing various diseases, with his medical officer Chi Po. Their discussions have come to be known as the *Nei Ching*, the oldest Chinese medical book.

There is no evidence that Hwang Ti himself discovered or developed the techniques he practiced. It is most likely that he only produced the first written record of a process of cultural development that had begun long before him. Indeed, the *Nei Ching* indicates that even Hwang Ti may have regarded his techniques as applications of ancient wisdom.

In the second chapter of the *Nei Ching*, entitled "Health and Longevity," there is a conversation in which Hwang Ti inquires of Chi Po: "I have heard that in ancient times, most people were still strong and vigorous after living a hundred years. Nowadays, many people are very weak even at age fifty. Why is this? Are the conditions of the times to be blamed, or are the people themselves different?" His medical officer answers that the ancients knew the Tao of health. They always followed the principle of yin and yang; their eating and drinking habits were moderate; they had regular schedules of action and rest; and they did not overwork or become exhausted. Therefore their bodies and spirits were in harmony, and they were able to attain the natural life span. Chi Po goes on to suggest that the wisdom of the ancients has become lost and that the people no longer live so long because their way of life has deteriorated.

As Chi Po's answer suggests, the practice of techniques for increasing longevity was far from a frivolous diversion for an idle monarch. Rather, it was regarded as having a significant effect on the quality as well as the length of life for those who practiced the techniques and also was considered an application of the fundamental principles of ancient Chinese philosophical wisdom.

Hwang Ti himself received many benefits as a result of his practices. It is not known exactly how long he lived, but his reign as emperor lasted a full century. According to legend, he became immortal and eventually rode off to heaven on the back of a dragon. In Shang Shi province, his tomb can be found, but it is said to contain only his shoes, which he dropped as the dragon flew away. The importance of Hwang Ti as a cultural and historical figure can hardly be overstated. Indeed, he is regarded as the ancestor of the entire Chinese nation. Every year near the beginning of April, the Chinese celebrate the holiday known as Ch'ing Ming (literally, "Clear and Bright"), which has a significance in some ways comparable to the Christian Good Friday and Easter. At this time, many people visit the tombs of their ancestors and honor the memory of Hwang Ti.

Centuries after the reign of Hwang Ti, the philosophical principles underlying the longevity techniques he practiced were articulated and developed by the great Taoist philosophers, particularly in the classics of Lao Tzu (6th century B.C.) and Chuang Tzu (4th century B.C.). Taoism eventually became, along with Confucianism and Buddhism, one of China's three great religions. It is unique among the world's major religions in its belief that personal immortality is possible and can, in principle if not often in actuality, be attained through the practice of its techniques. Several kinds of techniques have become highly refined over the centuries. The great British biochemist and historian Joseph Needham lists six kinds of Taoist techniques: respiratory, heliotherapeutic, gymnastic, sexual, alchemical and pharmaceutical, and dietary.[4]

The practice of Taoism has had varying importance in Chinese society at different times in history. During some periods, it had the approval of the emperor and became highly institutionalized. At other times, it was officially repressed and survived only in the unwritten traditions of the common folk. Regardless of its official status, however, it has survived as a continuous tradition since ancient times. Nearly every century has had at least one great Taoist physician. Some of them produced writings that provide us with a record of the development of Taoist health and longevity techniques. Perhaps the greatest of all was Sun Ssu Mo, who lived from A.D. 581 to 682. He is still widely esteemed by the Chinese today. Recently, both the People's Republic of China and the Nationalist Republic of China issued commemorative postage stamps in honor of his contribution to the prevention of smallpox. His writings, including the *Ch'ien Chin Fang* (A Thousand Ounces of Gold Prescriptions), are an extensive catalogue of diseases and prescribed cures and contain the earliest surviving written records of massage and acupressure techniques. In addition to massage, Sun Ssu Mo describes several kinds of longevity techniques, including breathing methods, calisthenics for various seasons and climates, sexual techniques, the use of food and herbs, and the cultivation and nourishment of the spirit. More information about Sun Ssu Mo will be found later in the book, in Chapter 9.

Another great Taoist whose writings are of importance was Chang Chun Fang, who lived during the Sung dynasty (10th–13th centuries A.D.). His book, *Yuen Chi Ch'i Chien* (Seven Categories for the Knowledge of the Clouds), is a codification of many earlier writings of Taoist masters and contains much more detail about the techniques of longevity than can be found in any previous single source. It is difficult to read, however, because the genuine information it contains is often mixed in with superstitious nonsense and talk about magic spells. The tendency of Taoism to become mixed with superstition and folk magic has had the unfortunate result that its central insights, expressed with such clear simplicity in the ancient classics, have often been obscured, and many people have failed to appreciate their real significance.

Yet another great Taoist of the Sung dynasty was Chang San Feng. He is credited with the development of the exercise method known as T'ai Chi Ch'uan, the ultimate refinement of T'u Na and Tao Yin techniques practiced by Hwang Ti.

The writings of the Ming dynasty (14th–17th centuries A.D.) include the *Eight Letters on Longevity* by Kao Lien. In addition to information on the kinds of techniques already mentioned, this book describes methods of planting and cultivating flowers, an activity that benefits the health by increasing the oxygen in the air breathed and also by promoting peace of mind. When practiced in conjunction with the kinds of Taoist techniques already mentioned, it can have remarkable results. The master Li Ch'ing Yuen, mentioned in the Preface, was born during the early Ching dynasty and was an herbalist by profession; at the time of his death in 1930, he was 250 years old.

Western medical authorities tend to be skeptical about claims of such great longevity as that of Li Ch'ing Yuen, even though in his case there is much supportive evidence. It should be remembered, however, that the study of gerontology and the development of geriatric techniques are very recent phenomena in Western culture. The knowledge of the aging process from the point of view of modern physical science is not highly advanced, and its technological application has been limited. Perhaps the best that could be claimed is that many of the diseases to which elderly people are susceptible have been found to be curable by chemical and medical treatments. Regarding the fundamental questions concerning the causes of aging itself and of the general physical deterioration that goes along with it, it is fair to say that these processes are not at all well understood on the molecular level. The chemistry involved has been found to be very complex, and no technique or method has been discovered that can prevent or retard the deterioration of aging.

By contrast, the Chinese have an ancient tradition that does not share the limitations of the Western approach. Taoist health and longevity practices, when performed correctly, affect all aspects of life, spiritual as well as physical. If they are made a regular part of daily life over a period of years, the deterioration of the body in old age can be prevented or at least greatly slowed down. Essential to the Chinese approach is the insight that healthy longevity is not just a problem for elderly people, but for the young as well, even for children. The best way to attain success is to establish favorable practices and habits early in life.

NOTES

1. *The Aging: Trends and Policies* (New York: United Nations, 1975).
2. Reported in the New York *Times*, September 9, 1977, p. A4.
3. Akira Ishihara and Howard S. Levy, trans., *The Tao of Sex* (New York: Harper and Row, 1968).
4. Joseph Needham, *Science and Civilization in China*, Vol. II (Cambridge: The University Press, 1954), p. 143.

CHAPTER 2:

HEALTH AND LONGEVITY IN THE WISDOM OF ANCIENT CHINA

Traditional Chinese religion is a mixture of concepts and practices derived from three main sources: Confucianism, Taoism, and Buddhism. The latter originated in India, was first introduced into China by missionaries in 305 B.C., and became influential during the Han dynasty. Taoism and Confucianism, on the other hand, originated in the philosophical thought of ancient China and have influenced the thinking as well as the daily lives of the Chinese people for more than 2,000 years. In recent times, their influence has been felt outside China and, indeed, throughout the world. Their classic writings have been translated into virtually every language. In English alone, there have been more than 100 translations of Lao Tzu's *Tao Te Ching* (Book of Tao).

In order to achieve genuine understanding of these ways of thought, one must realize that the major teachings of Taoism and Confucianism are significantly different from those of the great Western religions, as well as those of Buddhism. In the first place, they are not primarily concerned about God. Although the concept of Yin and Yang, the two fundamental cosmic forces, has a central role in Taoism, it cannot be regarded as a theological concept in the usual sense. The concept of God as a spirit, as a personal entity capable of purposeful action, as the creator of the world, or as affecting the course of human history is not to be found at all in Taoist or Confucianist thought. Secondly, they are not concerned with reincarnation or with the prospects of life after death, and lack the concepts of heaven and hell. This is not to say that they deny the spiritual aspect of human life, which, on the contrary, is of great importance in Taoism, as we will see. It is the idea of disembodied spirits that has no role.* The significant result of this is that Taoism and Confucianism do not share the tendency of many religions to find the ultimate solutions to the problems of this life in the promise of another life. The application of their wisdom is to be found in the concrete reality of daily life in this world, and their major concerns involve how to deal with the practical problems everyone encounters in the course of life. Among these are the concerns of health and longevity.

It is doubtful that the early Taoists and Confucianists actually regarded their teachings as religious. In both cases, these teachings represented a unified way of approaching a variety of scientific, philosophical, political, and ethical issues. The idea that they form a basis of a religion, in the sense of the organization of religious institutions and practices, evolved somewhat later in Chinese history (during the later Han Dynasty, around 156 A.D.). Both Taoism and Confucianism were fully developed as coherent philosophical viewpoints during the sixth century B.C., late in the Chou dynasty. In each case, this development was embodied in the life and work of a single great thinker: in the case of Taoism, Lao Tzu; in that of Confucianism, Con-

---

*Although life after death and ghosts are occasionally mentioned in the Taoist classics, such as the story in Chapter 18 of the *Sayings of Chuang Tzu*, in which Chuang Chou finds a human skull, and the ghost of its owner later appears to him in a dream and tells him about death and the afterlife, such passages must be considered metaphorical.

fucius. These two philosophical pioneers clearly formulated all the central ideas of the viewpoints they originated. Their writings are aphoristic in style and very concise, however, and would be quite difficult to understand were it not for the fact that each had a brilliant follower during the Period of the Warring States (403–221 B.C.) who wrote very detailed works commenting on and expanding the original ideas. Chuang Tzu, born in 370 B.C., created highly entertaining and often humorous writings in a free discursive style that explained Taoism in a manner fully consistent with the ideas of Lao Tzu. Meng Tzu, usually known in the West as Mencius, lived from 374 to 289 B.C.. He systematized and expanded the teachings of Confucius in his great works, which have been an invaluable source for the detailed study of Confucian thought ever since.

In this chapter, the main teachings of Taoism and Confucianism will be surveyed, insofar as they specifically relate to the concerns of health and longevity. To illustrate the ideas involved, a number of passages from the writings of these ancient philosophers will be discussed.[1]

TAOISM

The contribution of Taoist thought toward the understanding of longevity and how to attain good health comes about by direct application of its most central teachings. In fact, it is a major theme of the *Tao Te Ching*, the great classic by Lao Tzu.

Lao Tzu spent a good part of his early life as a civil servant, working as curator of the royal library of the state of Chou. In this capacity, it was his opportunity to study carefully the ancient writings, including many books and records that have since been lost or destroyed. After many years, he retired and went into seclusion in the Western mountains. It is not known when he died. According to one legend, he went to India and was involved in the origin of Buddhism.[2] Another legend is that he became an immortal and still lives alone in the high mountains. In any case, before going away he left behind a small work that brought together all the knowledge he had acquired after years of study and expressed all the essential features of the philosophy of Taoism. This writing came to be known as the *Tao Te Ching*, perhaps the most beautiful book ever written.

Several chapters of the *Tao Te Ching* concern the attainment of longevity through the process of rejuvenation. The relevant passages are interesting for their conception of the aims as well as the methods of this process. The following is taken from Chapter 10:

> When the spirit and the body are truly integrated, they can be kept from separating. When one concentrates the attention on fastening the spirit to the body and at the same time on the breathing (vitality), thereby attaining the utmost flexibility, he can become like a newborn baby.[3]

To appreciate the point of this passage, it is helpful to consider the following one from Chapter 55:

> He who attains true integration (the attributes of the Tao) is like a newborn baby. Poisonous insects will not sting him; birds of prey will not attack him. The baby's bones seem weak and his sinews soft, yet his grasp is strong. He knows nothing about the union of male and female,* yet his penis may some-

*Ignorance of the union between male and female is the subject of a humorous story in a famous Chinese novel *The Dream of the Red Chamber*, written during the Ch'ing dynasty by Ts'ao Hsueh Ch'in. According to the story, a young maidservant (whose nickname, Sa Ta Chieh, means "Innocent Girl") found an elegant ornamental purse embroidered with a pornographic picture. She was surprised about her find, and shouted it to her mistress, "Look! Fighting monsters!"

times become erect, revealing the perfection of his vital essence. Although he may cry all day long, he never becomes hoarse, showing his attainment of perfect harmony. He who understands this harmony knows the secret of unchanging vitality. He who knows the unchanging is enlightened.[4]

According to these quoted passages, the aim of the rejuvenation process is the achievement of perfect integration between the physical and spiritual aspects of human life. If one can attain this, his life will be free from harm. The goal of this attainment is spoken of as becoming like a newborn baby. The idea is that, when we are born, our bodies and minds are naturally harmonious, and we are completely flexible and open to whatever we may experience. As we grow up, however, we are subject to many pressures and worries and, in order to deal with them, we become unnaturally sophisticated and, as a result, lose our flexibility, becoming rigid and unyielding. This creates tension between our physical and spiritual aspects, and we gradually lose our original integration, deteriorate, and eventually die. The process of rejuvenation is a way of restoring harmony, and thus preventing deterioration. It works by concentrating the attention on the breathing, thus taking the mind away from the pressures and worries of life, and also by increasing mental and physical flexibility through the practice of gentle exercises.

Other passages in the *Tao Te Ching* emphasize the importance of keeping the mind peaceful and free from the pressures and distractions of social life in order to restore inner harmony. This is the point of the following excerpt from Chapter 20:

Most people look satisfied and pleased, as if celebrating a festival or climbing the heights in springtime. I alone seem quiet and listless, without any apparent desires. . . . Most people seem to have plenty. I alone seem to lack. . . . Most people seem intelligent and wise. I alone seem stupid and dull. Most people appear useful. I alone seem worthless. I am different from other men, for only I value the Tao.[5]

In spite of what this passage may seem to imply out of context, it does not mean that one must become a total recluse, completely cut off from other people, in order to achieve rejuvenation. What it does say is that even though it may seem attractive to keep up with the pace of society, there is even greater, longer-lasting value in being different and concentrating on inner harmony. Many elderly people now suffer unhappiness because old age forces them to withdraw from activities they consider important and to spend a great deal of time alone. They should find great consolation by discovering for themselves Lao Tzu's insight that to be left out of things is not necessarily a hardship, but in a very deep sense, a benefit.

Another point mentioned in the quotation above concerns freedom from desires. This is expanded upon in other passages as well, such as the following from Chapter 46:

There is no mistake greater than that of being ambitious; there is no calamity greater than that of being discontented; there is no fault greater than the desire for riches. Therefore, true contentment is an enduring and unchanging happiness.[6]

Whoever is able to attain freedom from ambitions and desires can escape the tension that results from continually striving to satisfy them. He has no need to insist on his point of view. He is never disappointed. He is soft and yielding and can easily accept whatever situation may come to pass. The realization of this insight in one's daily life is close to the secret of longevity, for, as Lao Tzu observes in Chapter 76:

When a man is alive, his body is soft and flexible; when he is dead, it is hard and rigid. So it is with all things. Trees and

plants are soft and pliant when they are growing; when they
die they are dry and brittle. Thus, to be hard and rigid is the
way of death; to be soft and yielding is the way of life.[7]

After Lao Tzu, the most important figure in Taoist history is Chuang Tzu. His writings follow closely the ideas of
Lao Tzu but are much more detailed, containing many
stories and parables as well as accounts of conversations.
Because of their clear style, they have great literary value
in addition to being a source of information about Taoist
philosophy. Concerns of health and longevity are a major
topic in these writings, and relevant passages can be found
in nearly every chapter. Even the titles of many of the
thirty-three chapters, such as Chapter 1: "Enjoyment in
Untroubled Ease," Chapter 3: "Preservation of Life Takes
Precedence," and Chapter 19: "Full Understanding of
Life," reflect the emphasis on these concerns.

Chuang Tzu lived during a period of great political tur-
moil and rapid development in China. The structures of the
feudal society that had governed during the time of Lao
Tzu collapsed when the dukes who ruled the larger feudal
states began to conquer and annex the smaller ones. The
conquering dukes became kings, who constantly sought
further expansion of their realms. By the time of Chuang
Tzu, of more than 100 dukedoms, there remained seven
large states, which were continually at war with each
other. This era in Chinese history thus came to be known as
the Period of the Warring States. It continued until 221
B.C., when the king of Chin conquered the other states and
became emperor.

As a result of the intense competition between the
states, civilization developed more quickly than in any previous period and scholars were much in demand as the kings
hoped to achieve superiority over their rivals through the
wisdom and strategic advice of brilliant advisers. Chuang

Tzu himself was offered the position of prime minister in the state of Ch'u, but he refused to accept it. The account of the offer and his refusal is to be found in Chapter 17 of his writings, entitled "The Floods of Autumn." It is interesting for what it reveals about the Taoist attitude toward positions of high prestige and responsibility in society. The royal officials bearing the king's offer came upon Chuang Tzu while he was fishing in the Pu river. Upon hearing the offer, he compared himself to a tortoise, saying that he would rather continue to drag his tail through the mud than die and have his shell kept in a place of honor in the king's ancestral temple.[8] The point is that high positions carry with them a great burden of problems and worries. Those who hold them inevitably suffer personal stress and lose the freedom to attain harmony with nature. Thus burdened, they are likely to die prematurely, unable to benefit from the honors that are bestowed on them posthumously. In order to attain health and longevity, it is better to give up such positions and simply "drag one's tail through the mud"—that is, live a completely free life, with neither public significance nor worrisome responsibilities. This wisdom has direct application in the lives of many elderly people, since it shows how to look upon retirement not as a loss but as a great benefit.

Chuang Tzu's indifference toward power and prestige is typical of his attitude toward the other values people commonly strive for. In Chapter 18 of his writings, entitled "Perfect Happiness," the discussion concerns whether there really exists such a thing as perfect happiness. He observes that people generally assume that it involves the fulfillment of their desires and the avoidance of pain. Thus they urgently work toward such things as riches, skills, honors, longevity, security, an abundance of good food, fine clothing, beautiful things to look at, and pleasing music. Unfortunately, there seems to be inevitable disappoint-

ment in such striving. Even if some desires are ful-
filled, others remain empty, and become a source of worry
and confusion. Chuang Tzu expresses his own view as follows:

> Regarding what people commonly do today and what gives
> them joy, I am not sure whether that joy is really joy or not. I
> see them pursuing all their aims automatically, as if they had
> no other choice. But what they regard as joy would not be so to
> me, yet I do not claim that there is no joy in it. Is there such a
> thing as true joy or not? To me, doing nothing (perfect free-
> dom) seems to be true joy, but people ordinarily consider it a
> waste. Thus it is said: "Perfect joy gives no thought to joy; the
> highest praise gives no thought to praise."[9]

From this passage we can see that Chuang Tzu, like Lao
Tzu, refrains from pursuing all the commonly esteemed
values and instead seeks freedom and peace of mind.
Another important aspect of his philosophy is also revealed
in the quotation, namely the idea that many things that
seem inevitable or absolutely true about the world are actually relative to a temporary point of view and subject to
change. As a result of this view, Chuang Tzu generally
regards it as pointless to argue about questions of right and
wrong or about what may be profitable or harmful, for the
answers to such questions can only be given relative to
changing situations and viewpoints. Thus the person with
true wisdom is not concerned about such distinctions. He
does not need to worry about unexpected changes and can
accept whatever may occur without sadness or disappoint-
ment. Chuang Tzu tells several stories that illustrate the
benefits of this philosophy, such as how it enabled him to
accept the death of his wife with equanimity and without
sadness, and how it enabled Mr. Deformed and Mr. Loose
Mind not to worry about their tumors.[10] Another parable
shows that even fear of death can be overcome by application of the same idea.

How do I know that love of life is not a delusion? How do I know that dislike of death is not like a child's becoming lost and not realizing that he is really returning home? Li Chi was a daughter of the chief of Ai. When the ruler of Ch'in first captured her, she wept until her dress was wet with tears. But when she arrived at the palace, slept with the king, and ate his grass-and-grain-fed meat, she regretted that she had wept. How do I know that the dead do not similarly repent their earlier desire for life?[11]

A similar point is made through the story mentioned earlier in this chapter, in which a skull found by Chuang Tzu later appeared to him in a dream at midnight, offering to tell him about death:

In death there are no distinctions between ruler and servant. There are none of the phenomena of the changing seasons. We pass our time in ease and tranquility. . . . No king in his court has greater joys than the dead.[12]

The point of these stories is not to promise a heaven hereafter. Rather than as a literal prediction of a form of life after death, the words of the skull should be regarded as a description of the Taoist view of utopia, the surrounding tale of the finding of the skull and the subsequent dream being understood as a literary device. The purpose of the story, like that of the previously quoted one, is to emphasize that the view of death available to the living is quite limited and temporary. All we know definitely about it is that it is a natural process, a kind of change. Rather than confronting it with apprehension, fear, or other expectations, the person with true wisdom simply accepts it, whatever it may turn out to be, and thereby achieves peace of mind, tranquility, and the resulting benefits of a healthy old age.

The phenomenon of dreaming was of great interest to Chuang Tzu, and not merely as a storytelling device. In a

deeply reflective passage, which immediately follows the
story of Li Chi in Chapter 2, he finds in it a profound insight
regarding the distinction between appearance and reality.

> Those who dream of drinking wine may weep the next morn-
> ing. Those who dream of weeping may enjoy hunting the next
> morning. During their dreams they are not aware that they
> are dreaming, but only after waking up do they understand
> that they have been dreaming. Sometime there will be a great
> awakening, and we will then realize that this life is merely a
> big dream. Meanwhile, the stupid think they are already
> awake. Insisting on their limited knowledge, they think they
> can tell the difference between rulers and herdsmen. What
> prejudice! Confucius and you are both dreaming, and my tell-
> ing you that you are dreaming is also merely a dream.[13]

The point here is that once we notice that a dream may be
vivid enough that the dreamer does not realize that he is
not awake, we must admit the possibility that our entire
experience, including all we regard as true and real, is
nothing but a figment of our dreaming imagination. There
is nothing within our experience that can guarantee to us,
as we experience it, that it is waking rather than dream
experience. The consequences of this realization cut deeply
into the ordinary notion of reality, for it casts into doubt
virtually all beliefs about the world.

Two millennia after Chuang Tzu, this insight was rediscovered by the French philosopher René Descartes and,
through his writings,[14] had a deep influence on modern
Western philosophy. Descartes found the insight to be a
source of worry and confusion, since it meant that he could
not trust his perceptions to provide evidence for the truth.
Chuang Tzu, on the other hand, drawing a similar conclusion, took the opposite attitude. His view is that the real
source of worry and confusion is the apparently real world,
with all its pressures and entanglements. The truly wise

person, realizing that these may well be an illusion, does not take them too seriously. Thus he is free to achieve harmony with nature however it may be. He does not need to worry about obtaining true knowledge about the state of the world.

Throughout his writings, Chuang Tzu again and again emphasizes the importance of a peaceful attitude toward life. Even in working toward the aims of health and longevity through the use of Taoist exercises and other techniques such as those described in this book, a tranquil spirit is more essential than the practices themselves. If they are performed impatiently, or if we are anxious for quick results, the techniques will not have their beneficial effects. As Chuang Tzu puts it in Chapter 15:

> If one is interested in a good character without tormenting the mind, in self-improvement without propriety and self-righteousness, in successful government service without spectacular deeds and fame, in enjoyment of leisure without going to beach or river resorts, in longevity without breathing or stretching exercises, then one forgets all things, yet possesses all things. When one has become completely free, all fine things come one's way. Such men pursue the way of nature, and display true wisdom. Thus it is said, "Placidity, indifference, silence, quietude, emptiness, and inaction: these are the attributes which constitute the stability of nature and the essence of the Tao."[15]

In order to understand this quotation correctly, we must be careful in interpreting it. At first glance, it seems to say that breathing and movement exercises such as those described in this book are unnecessary for good health, that it is sufficient to maintain a certain mental attitude toward life. In a way, this is true. However, the context of the quotation makes clear that such a conclusion applies literally only at the most advanced stage of the practice of

Taoism, in which the exercises become an unnecessary hindrance. In the earlier stages, and certainly at the beginning, it is essential to have a proper balance that includes both the practice of regular exercises and the realization of a peaceful, worry-free attitude through reflective insight. It is good to keep in mind the warning of Carl Jung, who after studying the Taoist classics carefully for many years, observed that they would be a "poison for the Western mind," since the Western tendency merely to study words instead of actually experiencing their content would reduce the Taoist teachings to a dangerous ideology.[16]

An example that shows the insufficiency of an overly intellectual response to Taoism can be found in the life of a well-known American academician who specialized in Eastern philosophy. Though he was an expert on Taoist philosophy, famous for his lectures and writings on the subject, whose skill in the Chinese language and calligraphy exceeded that of many Chinese, he did not benefit from the practical application of the Taoist health methods, and died of a heart attack at the age of 55.

But one can avoid the dangers of an overly intellectual approach and realize the full benefit of Taoist wisdom by treating it neither as a pure ideology nor as a pure technique but as a properly balanced way of living one's whole life. The concept of "balance" is thus crucial for the successful application of the various theoretical aspects. "Balance" is also an important topic in ancient Chinese philosophy, especially in the writing of the Confucianist school, as we will see in the next section.

CONFUCIANISM

The influence of Confucius on Chinese civilization can scarcely be overestimated. He attained some significance as a politician, and his achievements as a scholar included editing the ancient classics, but his main importance resulted from his teaching. The philosophy of Confucianism, which came to affect virtually all aspects of Chinese society, resulted from the efforts of many generations of his students, who worked to expand and develop further the teachings of the master. It is sometimes difficult for Westerners to appreciate the full importance of Confucianism in China, especially when they hear or read about Chinese leaders criticizing its fundamental ideas. In recent times, the Communists have attacked Confucius as an aristocrat whose teachings protected the interests of powerful feudal bureaucrats, calling Confucianism a "poison for the people's minds" and a great hindrance to the progress of society. Such charges have been heard in China many times before, even in antiquity, from revolutionary groups who wished to overthrow the established government. But, to keep these criticisms in their proper perspective, one must realize that they concern the political implications of Confucianist thought, but that many other aspects of Confucianism are unaffected by them and have abiding value in Chinese life. Among these are the teachings concerning health, especially those relating to the concepts of *chung* (equilibrium) and *yung* (persistence without change.)

Kung Fu Tzu (Confucius) lived for 73 years, from 552 until 479 B.C.; thus he was a contemporary of Lao Tzu. He descended from an old family with a long tradition of civil service. His father was minister of state in the Tso district. Early in his life, he worked as a legal official in the state of Lu and for a brief period served as acting prime minister. He was soon ousted from political power, however, and subsequently spent several years traveling throughout China seeking a position of influence, often suffering from starvation and other hardships. Later on he returned to his home state of Lu, concentrated on teaching and scholarship, and achieved respect and fame. His students became high officials throughout China, and his school eventually became so important that to study there was a necessary prerequisite for an important government position.

In his teaching, Confucius emphasized the physical and social aspects of life. He was not given to religious or metaphysical speculations. His attitude toward such topics is typified by the following passage from the *Analects*, a book that mainly records his teachings and dialogues with his students.

> One of his students, Chi Lu, asked about serving God and the ghosts of the dead. The Master said, "When you cannot even serve human beings, how can you serve those things?" Chi Lu persisted, "But I wish to know about death." He was answered, "When you do not even know about life, how can you know about death?"[17]

Confucius' attitude on this was maintained for centuries by his followers. Chu Hsi, a great neo-Confucian of the Sung dynasty (12th century A.D.), made a particularly strong statement about it:

> Someone asked whether, at the time of death, a man's consciousness is dissipated and scattered. The philosopher added that it was not merely dissipated, but completely finished. The *chi* (of his body) comes to an end, and so does his consciousness.[18]

Confucius' teachings on the subject of health consist mainly of items of practical advice for application in everyday life. These he communicated to his students as much by his own example as by words. The *Analects* contains descriptions of his regular habits regarding food, clothing, sleep, and so on. In Book X, Chapter 8,[19] several dietary practices are mentioned. For example, he did not eat rice, meat, or fish that was discolored, spoiled, badly cooked, or out of season. He ate meat only when served with a sauce and did not eat too much of it, keeping a proper balance between amounts of meat and rice. He drank wine, but never so much that it made him drunk, and avoided the wine as well as cooked meat bought in the market, preferring home-made. He often used ginger to spice his food. He did not eat too much or too fast and did not talk while eating. Chapter 6 of the same book[20] describes his habits of dress. He generally dressed for comfort and convenience and avoided bright and gaudy colors. For social occasions, such as appearances at court or visits of condolence, he was careful to dress respectfully and in accordance with custom. His sleeping habits are described in various places.[21] It is reported, for example, that he did not sleep stretched out on his back like a corpse, but curled up, using his bent arm as a pillow.

The Confucianist philosophy is almost exclusively concerned with its application in human affairs, however. Chapter 1 describes how it pertains to the mind:

> While there are no stirrings of pleasure, anger, sorrow or joy, the mind may be said to be in a state of equilibrium. . . . This equilibrium is the great root from which grow all the human acts in the world.[22]

This passage is interesting because it sounds quite similar to various Taoist sayings that advocate peace of mind and avoidance of strong emotions, thus indicating that although Taoism and Confucianism were generally quite opposite philosophical viewpoints in ancient times, some of the fundamental concepts from which they evolved are similar. This helps to explain how it was possible for later Chinese religious experience to synthesize aspects of both.

The practical advice of Confucius regarding these and

other matters is based on a coherent way of viewing life that can be applied in many ways. The writings of Confucius himself do not expound the theory underlying this point of view, but several of his students and followers wrote theoretical works that do. An important early theoretical writing is *The Doctrine of the Mean*, composed by Tsze-sze, who was Confucius' grandson. It introduces two concepts that may be regarded as a basis for many of the practical rules of Confucianism. These are the concepts of *chung* and *yung*.

Chung is defined as "equilibrium" or "being without inclination to either side." In the first chapter of *The Doctrine of the Mean*, it is said to be "the correct course to be pursued by all under heaven."[23] Thus it should be regarded as applying to all of nature as well as human activities.

Several of the health practices of Confucius mentioned earlier can be understood as simple applications of the principle of *chung*. Thus, for example, he did not refrain from the pleasures of food (including spices) and drink (including wine), but enjoyed them in moderation. He dressed for comfort and convenience, but not so as to appear unusual or disrespectful of others. In general, he sought to achieve balance between extremes, and to avoid excess.

The concept of *yung* can be understood in relation to that of *chung*. Literally, "yung" means "persistence, or continuing, without change." In Confucianist theory, it refers to perseverence in the ways of virtue. This idea can also be found in Chapter 1 of *The Doctrine of the Mean:*[24]

> The path may not be left for an instant. If it could be left, it would not be the path. Therefore, the superior person does not wait until he sees things to be cautious, nor till he hears things to be apprehensive.

Among the virtues to which this principle pertains are those relating to health. In fact, it is essential to apply it in order to enjoy the benefits of health and longevity through the methods described in this book. The point is that good health practices, whether they involve exercise, meditation, or diet, do not have their beneficial effects on a particular occasion or after a short period of intense effort. They work only after becoming regular habits of life. The formation of such habits is accomplished through *yung*.

The full flowering of Confucianist philosophy is to be found in the writings of Meng Tzu (Mencius), second only to Confucius as a Confucian sage. Like his Taoist counterpart, Chuang Tzu, he lived during the Period of the Warring States. As a young man he was a student of Tsze-sze, and became thoroughly acquainted with the teachings of Confucius. Tsze-sze eventually entrusted Mencius with his own writings, including *The Doctrine of the Mean*. For many years, Mencius lived in the state of Ch'i; and though not of noble birth, he held the position of Ch'ing, guest consultant to the king, with rank equivalent to that of a duke. The state of Ch'i was the richest and most civilized of the Chinese states, a center of learning of all kinds, and so Mencius was influenced by the ideas of many schools in addition to those of Confucius. As a result, his writings represent a significant expansion and further development of Confucianist thought.

The remarkable history of Ch'i as a center of civilization in ancient China began in pre-Confucian times. In 685 B.C., a great statesman, philosopher, and influence on Taoist thought, Kuan Chung, became prime minister. He saw that the location of Ch'i along the seaboard was advantageous for the success of shipping and commercial enterprises, and also for the production of salt. Thus his policies emphasized economic development, including the production of salt and iron. By the time of his death in 645 B.C., Ch'i was on its way to becoming the wealthiest state in China.

Fortunately for the rulers and rich merchants of Ch'i, it had yet another advantage in its sometimes warlike competition with its neighbors. It was superior to all the other states in its development and use of military strategy. Its generals included the great Sun Wu Tzu, whose theoretical writing, the *Sun Tzu*, is even today considered the most important book ever written on military strategy and has been translated into many Western languages. Later on in the Warring States period, people came to Ch'i from every state in China to study military science. The school of Wang Shu, the mysterious sage who composed the *Kuei Ku Tzu* (Book of the Devil Valley Master), instructed students not only in military methods, but also in political science and philosophy, including meditation and techniques of health and longevity. Several of Wang Shu's students later became famous generals and political strategists. These included both of the leaders who shaped the major alliances among the states that affected the eventual outcome of the Warring States period. In addition to the state of Ch'i, the most powerful state was Ch'in, which occupied a large territory in the west. It was separated from the other six states by the Han Ku Kwan mountains. These six states, including Ch'i, extended from north to south beside the sea in the east. Su Ch'in, the prime minister of Ch'i, a student of Wang Shu, persuaded the six eastern states to form an alliance to cooperate in protecting themselves against Ch'in. This was called the Vertical Alliance, and Su Ch'in was its joint premier. Later on, however, another student of Wang Shu, Chang Yi, who was prime minister of Ch'in, persuaded some of the states to desert the Vertical Alliance, and to form a new alliance with Ch'in. This was the Horizontal Alliance. It was among the factors contributing to the ultimate victory of Ch'in over Ch'i, and the origin of the Ch'in empire in 221 B.C.

But the state of Ch'i was a center for many other kinds of

ideas and learning besides military and political strategy. The great naturalist and founder of the Yin-Yang school, Tsou Yen, also lived and taught there. Eventually the state established and built an academy of advanced study and research, the Ch'i Shia, which attracted scholars of many different schools from every state in China.[25]

Thus Meng Tzu, during his years as a respected adviser to the king of Ch'i, had plenty of opportunity to discuss and argue with as well as be influenced by people whose ideas where quite different from those of Confucius. As a result, although he remained consistent with Confucian principles, his writings show not only elaboration and a more precise statement of the simple teachings of the Master but also a genuine expansion of Confucianist philosophy. Most importantly, he went beyond Confucius in being concerned not only with the physical and social aspects of life but also with the spiritual.

A passage exemplifying this concern with the spiritual is the following, from Book VII of *The Works of Mencius:*

> To preserve one's mind and to nourish one's spirit is the way to serve nature (heaven). When a man realizes that there is no real difference between a short lifetime and a long one, and does not worry, but waits, cultivating his own personal character, for whatever may come to pass—this is the way he carries out his fate-(heaven)-ordained being.[26]

This quotation is interesting because it shows both how closely Mencius follows the Confucian tradition and how influenced he is by other ideas, especially Taoist ones. On the one hand, in talking about the cultivation of the personal character, he relies on the traditional Confucian teaching, as explained in the following quotation from *The Great Learning*, another early Confucianist work:

What is meant by "The cultivation of the personal character

depends on rectifying the mind" may be thus illustrated: If a man is under the influence of passion, he will be incorrect in his conduct. He will be the same, if he is under the influence of terror, or under the influence of fond regard, or under that of sorrow and distress.[27]

This quotation in turn harks back to the passage quoted earlier from the *Doctrine of the Mean*, which explains the application of *chung* to the mind. On the other hand, the quotation from Mencius also shows a distinct Taoist influence, perhaps echoing Chuang Tzu, who writes in his chapter on "Making All Things Equal,"[28] "There is no one more long-lived than a child who dies prematurely."

Indeed, in advocating the virtues of peace of mind, freedom from worry, and avoidance of strong passions, Mencius adopts a favorite Taoist theme. To be sure, when he talks about the consequences of keeping the mind at peace or having it clouded by emotions, he speaks in terms of "correct" and "incorrect" action. This shows a typical Confucianist emphasis on morality. A Taoist would emphasize instead the consequences for health and longevity. But though the emphasis differs, the advice is the same in practice.

Throughout the *Works of Mencius*, there are many other passages that suggest Taoist influence, such as his saying, "To nourish the mind there is nothing better than to make the desires few."[29] Perhaps the most remarkable are those in which Mencius explains his theory of the two distinct components of the human spirit: the will or mind and the *chi* (vitality). The following excerpt is from Book II:

The will is the leader (commander) of the *chi* (vitality). The vitality pervades the body and moves it. The will is of primary importance; the vitality is secondary. Therefore I say: Maintain a firm will and do not harm the vitality. . . . When the will is concentrated, it moves the vitality. When the vitality is concentrated, it moves the will. The latter occurs, for example, when a man runs or falls down: the vitality is violent and moves the mind. . . . I am skillful at nourishing my Great Grand Vitality.[30]

When asked by a student to define what is meant by "Great Grand Vitality," Mencius replies, "It is difficult to describe it. The vitality is very great and very strong. If it is nourished and not harmed, it fills up everything between heaven and earth (the whole body). . . . Without it, a man dies."[31]

To make sense of this quotation, one should keep in mind that we are using the word "vitality" to translate the word *chi*. The full significance of this Chinese word is hard to express in a single English phrase. It signifies vital energy and also respiration, including both the breathing and the circulation of blood that carries the breath throughout the body, and has a spiritual connotation as well. The remarkable thing is that what Mencius says regarding the *chi* combines all these aspects in a way that applies accurately to the practice of Taoist exercises such as T'ai Chi Ch'uan. In the correct practice of such exercises, the conscious mind concentrates on the *chi*, which in turn propels and moves the arms and legs. This leads to increased awareness of the flow of the *chi* throughout the entire body, improving circulation and resulting in increased energy. Thus it is written in the T'ai Chi Ch'uan classic, in the chapter entitled "Thirteen Forms with Mind Movement": "Use the mind to direct the *chi*. . . . Use the *chi* to propel the body."

The fact that this process is accurately described in virtually the same words in a writing of the Confucianist tradition shows that the T'ai Chi Ch'uan exercises are actually a great synthesis of the ancient wisdom of China. They represent a refinement of a long tradition of Taoist techniques of health and longevity, and at the same time realize the Confucianist ideal of nourishing the spirit.

The ideal of nourishing the spirit as well as the body is central to the teachings of Mencius. Thus in Book VI, Chapter 8, he writes, "If it receives its proper nourishment, there is nothing that will not grow. If it loses its proper nourishment, there is nothing which will not decay."[32] By applying this principle in his own life, Mencius was able to live to the age of eighty-four, more than a decade longer than Confucius. Other students and followers of Confucius who perhaps equaled Mencius in their understanding of philosophy were not as successful in achieving longevity. In fact, Yen Hui, who was Confucius' favorite student,[33] died when he was only thirty-two, having become sick as a result of a long period of undernourishment. It is hoped that the readers of this book will be able to use the ideas and techniques it describes in such a way as to obtain a proper balance of physical and spiritual nourishment, and thereby to enjoy long and healthy lives.

NOTES

1. The translations of passages from the ancient classics quoted in this and other chapters are my own. I have occasionally benefited by consulting other translations, especially those of the great nineteenth-century scholar James Legge. For each quotation I supply a source note in which I cite the page number of the corresponding passage in the Legge translation. Although I do not always agree with his wording, interested readers thus will be able to check the context of each quoted passage if they wish. In order to make the source notes concise, I employ abbreviations in referring to Legge's works. These are as follows: CC=*The Chinese Classics*, in five volumes (Hong Kong: Hong Kong University Press, 1960), vol. I: "Confucian Analects," "The Great Learning," "The Doctrine of the Mean"; vol. II: "The Works of Mencius." TT=*The Texts of Taoism*, in two volumes (New York: Dover Publications, 1962), vol. I: "The Tao Te Ching of Lao Tzu," "The Writings of Chuang Tzu," chapters 1–17; vol. II: "The Writings of Chuang Tzu," chapters 18–33.

2. Joseph Needham, *Science and Civilization in China*, vol. II (Cambridge: The University Press, 1954), p. 159.

3. For other translations, see Legge, TT, vol. I, p. 53; and Ch'u To Kao, *Tao Te Ching* (New York: Samuel Weiser, 1973), p. 22.

4. For other translations, see Legge, TT, vol. I, p. 99; Needham, *Science and Civilization*, vol. II, p. 140; and Ch'u To Kao, p. 70.

5. See Legge, TT, vol. I, pp. 62–63.

6. See *ibid.*, p. 89.

7. See *ibid.*, p. 118.

8. See *ibid.*, p. 390.

9. *Ibid.*, vol. II, p. 3.

10. *Ibid.*, pp. 4 and 5.

11. *Ibid.*, vol. I, p. 194.

12. *Ibid.*, vol. II, p. 6.

13. *Ibid.*, vol. I, pp. 194–195.

14. It is to be found in both of Descartes's major philosophical writings: in Part IV of the *Discourse on Method*, written in 1637, as well as in the first of the six *Meditations on First Philosophy*, 1641. See *The Philosophical Works of Descartes*, trans. E. S. Haldane and G. R. T. Ross (Cambridge: The University Press, 1967), vol. I, pp. 101 and 145–46.

15. See Legge, TT, vol. I. pp. 364–65.

16. See his letter to Dr. Chang Chuan-yuan in *C. G. Jung's Letters* (Princeton, N.J.: Princeton University Press, 1973), vol. I, pp. 559–60. Jung writes: "If one could arrive at the truth by learning the words of wisdom, then the world would have been saved already in the remote times of Lao-Tzu. . . . wisdom cannot be taught by words. It is only possible by personal contact and immediate experience."

17. See Legge, CC, vol. I, pp. 240–41.

18. Chu Tze, *Ch'uan Shu*, chap. 51, here quoted from Needham, *Science and Civilization*, vol. II, p. 490.

19. See Legge, CC, vol. I, p. 232.

20. *Ibid.*, pp. 230–31.

21. *Ibid.*, pp. 200, 235.

22. *Ibid.*, p. 384.

23. *Ibid.*, p. 382.

24. *Ibid.*, p. 384.

25. See Needham, *Science and Civilization*, vol. II, pp. 233–34.

26. See Legge, CC, vol. II, p. 449.

27. *Ibid.*, vol. I, p. 368.

28. See Legge, TT, vol. I, p. 188.

29. See Legge, CC, vol. II, p. 497.

30. See *ibid.*, pp. 188–89.

31. See *ibid.*, p. 190.

32. See *ibid.*, p. 409.

33. See the *Analects*, Book VI, Chapter 2, in *ibid.*, vol. I, p. 185.

CHAPTER 3:

T'AI CHI CH'UAN AND THE SYSTEMS OF THE BODY

T'AI CHI CH'UAN AND HEALTH

T'ai Chi Ch'uan is a self-relaxing exercise whose slow, even movements are coordinated with breathing and directed by a peaceful mind. Thus it is beneficial to both mental and physical health. The famous master Yearning K. Chen explains that T'ai Chi Ch'uan rids all parts of the body of spiritual and physical defects, clears the mind and strengthens the brain, and promotes good digestion and sound kidneys.[1] T'ai Chi Ch'uan exercises also help to lower high blood pressure, soften blood vessels, and regulate the circulation of the blood.

It is not surprising then that many people with various ailments have shown remarkable improvement after taking up T'ai Chi Ch'uan. Some have even gone on to become T'ai Chi Ch'uan masters themselves. Such is the case, for example, of Y. T. Liu who began practicing the exercise in his sixties because of heart disease.[2] His illness was gone after a year; and, now Liu, who is in his 80s and still in good health, teaches T'ai Chi on both coasts of the United States.

I, through years of practicing and teaching, have come to realize that T'ai Chi Ch'uan is effective for all systems of the body and that it not only prevents but also cures sicknesses and disabilities.

THE CENTRAL NERVOUS SYSTEM

The central nervous system, which extends from the base of the back to the brain, is the most important system in the body. It receives information from outside and inside the body. It transmits the body's actions and reactions to the brain and directs the movements of the limbs and the sense organs. The central nervous system will only remain in good condition and function properly if we keep the spinal column erect.

The spinal column is important because it is the frame that supports the body much as a central beam supports a house. It is composed of a series of vertebrae, and it encloses the spinal cord. As a person grows older, the spaces between the vertebrae shorten because of pressure, causing the spinal cord to shrink and one's posture to stoop. Indirectly, this pressure can damage the inner organs—possibly causing tuberculosis or heart disease. It may even impair the eyesight.

Keeping the spinal column erect is the first step toward rejuvenating the body. The spinal columns of children are naturally erect, but those of older people are more bent because of bad habits. Methods to correct this condition will be discussed in a later chapter. For the moment it is important to keep in mind that, according to the T'ai Chi Ch'uan classics, vitality and blood circulation are transmitted from the lower body to the brain when the spinal column is kept erect.

THE DIGESTIVE SYSTEM

A second key to good health and long life is a healthy digestive system. The digestive system stores and supplies all nourishment for the body. When it functions properly, we get enough nutrition from the food we ingest. Good digestion affects calorie usage, the digestion of food, and the excretion of wastes. However, faulty digestion prevents needed nutrients from reaching the organs of the body. Undigested food acts upon the stomach and the intestines, causing many ailments. Cramps, indigestion, and constipation are minor disorders that occur when the digestive system is not in good condition. More serious illnesses—such as gastric ulcers and stomach cancer—can only be treated by surgery.

Several movements of the T'ai Chi Ch'uan form, which are described in detail in Chapter 5 below, are especially beneficial to the digestive system. These include the movements known as Single Whip, Play Guitar, and White Crane Spreads Wings. What is characteristic of these movements is that they expand and contract the body in an opening and closing motion. In so doing, they vibrate and stimulate the stomach and intestines. Even though the digestive system is involuntary, it can be affected by breathing that is directed by the mind.

THE RESPIRATORY SYSTEM

Third in importance to health and longevity is the respiratory system. Food is vital to sustaining life, but breathing is even more essential. To go without food for a few days causes discomfort but is not fatal. However, to stop breathing for only one minute is very serious and, if prolonged for several minutes, causes death. All living things—even plants—rely on breathing for life. Meditators and practitioners of the martial arts cannot achieve their goals without correct breathing. In T'ai Chi Ch'uan exercises, breathing is valued more than physical power. As gas propels a machine, breathing—not muscular strength—propels the movements of T'ai Chi Ch'uan. At the same time, the movements act like a bellows to help the breathing: When the movement is "open," more fresh air comes in; when "closed," more air is exhaled.

Most Westerners think that "deep breathing" means filling the lungs with air and holding their breath. In T'ai Chi Ch'uan, the correct meaning of "deep breathing" is directing the inhaled air down into the trunk of the body. For example, children breathe through their abdomens, but as people, especially in the West, get older they limit their breathing to the lungs. As a result, the lungs often enlarge and crowd the heart, causing heart disease. People who are elderly or very ill breathe even more shallowly, limiting breath to the throat.

In T'ai Chi Ch'uan, the word for breathing *(chi)* means not only the air that is inhaled and exhaled but also the spirit and intrinsic energy derived from the *tan t'ien*, the psychic center of the body, which is located about three inches below the navel. The mind directs the *chi*, letting it sink down into the abdomen, thereby penetrating even to the bones.

THE CIRCULATORY SYSTEM

Connected to the respiratory system is the circulatory

system. Blood cannot move itself: It is guided by the *chi*. When breathing stops, blood circulation stops also. T'ai Chi Ch'uan movement guides the *chi* so that more oxygen enters the blood. With continuous, slow motion, fresh blood cleans, repairs, and nourishes every part of the body.

If the breathing is not deep enough, fresh blood can only go to limited places. In many parts of the body—such as the face and the hands—blood vessels are as thin as hair. When fresh blood does not reach these blood vessels, they cannot assimilate. Like a flower that does not get water and fertilizer, they wither. As a result, the face and hands appear older and the body is more susceptible to sickness. When T'ai Chi Ch'uan is performed regularly and correctly, fresh blood circulates to these thin blood vessels. It makes the body strong and prolongs youth.

In the circulatory system, two components of the blood that contribute to good health are the red and white blood cells. The red blood cells nourish and clean the tissues of the body. The oxygen we breathe is carried to all the organs and systems of the body by the red blood cells. They then carry carbon dioxide from the body tissues to the lungs and waste products to the excretory organs. The white blood cells carry antibodies through the bloodstream that destroy harmful bacteria and repair damaged body tissue. These red and white blood cells are like the Taoist concepts of Yin and Yang, two polar forces that must be balanced. If there are not enough white blood cells, the body cannot defend itself against infection and disease; not enough red blood cells causes anemia and leukemia. The slow, even movements of T'ai Chi Ch'uan maintain the balance between red and white blood cells. By regulating the circulation, T'ai Chi Ch'uan movements and deep breathing prevent high blood pressure as well.

THE ENDOCRINE SYSTEM

The glands of the endocrine system control the organs of the body by releasing secretions called hormones. Some secretions pass through ducts, such as saliva in the mouth, which aids digestion. Other endocrine glands are ductless, secreting their hormones directly into the bloodstream. The blood carries these hormones to all of the body's organs, affecting their growth and activity. Thus, the endocrine glands directly influence many of the processes important to life, including growth, sexual maturation, reproduction, and aging. There are many glands in the body. We shall only select those that relate to T'ai Chi Ch'uan and longevity.

THE PITUITARY GLAND AND THE PINEAL BODY

The pituitary gland is only about one centimeter in diameter. However, it exerts a controlling influence on the other endocrine glands. Its hormones affect skin pigmentation, the protein in long bones, and the maturation of male and female sex organs. The pituitary hormones also stimulate the thyroid and adrenal glands. The posterior lobe of the pituitary stores hormones secreted by the hypothalamus. Among these are pituitrin which is a hormone that reduces urine by acting on the kidneys and also lowers blood pressure. Attached to the mid-brain, the pineal body is even smaller than the pituitary gland. In Western medicine, the endocrine function of the pineal is unknown. Chinese Taoists, however, believe that the pituitary and the pineal have two functions: One controls the acceleration of sexual growth, while the other retards the aging process.

The Taoist concept *huan ching pu nuo*, implicit in the movements of T'ai Chi Ch'uan, is believed to help both the pituitary gland and the pineal body function properly. Taoists believe that the vitality of the sperm can be purified into a source of energy.[3] *Huan ching pu nuo* is the Taoist term for directing this vitality from the lower body to the brain.

An excellent T'ai Chi Ch'uan movement that applies this principle is called Step Back and Repulse Monkey. At the beginning of this movement, the right hand drops to the thigh area as you step back with the right foot and inhale. As the right hand moves back and rises to the head area, the mind and the *chi* carry the vitality from the *tan t'ien* in the abdomen through the spinal cord to the brain. Now the right hand pushes forward and away from the head area, while you exhale. This causes your mind to bring the energy from the brain through the mouth to the front of the body and return it to the *tan t'ien*. This exercise brings vitality to the pituitary gland and the pineal body.

THE THYROID GLAND

The thyroid gland, located in the neck, stores most of the body's supply of iodine. Its hormones increase the rate of oxidation in the body (producing heat) and of the sugar metabolism. Furthermore, the thyroid hormones stimulate the central nervous system, the adrenals and gonads, and the development of bones and teeth. As such, the thyroid gland affects the physical growth of the body.

A serious disease of the thyroid gland is goiter. This occurs when an iodine deficiency causes swelling of the gland. In the West, physicians treat goiter with medicines and surgery. But the Chinese use the movements of T'ai Chi Ch'uan as a preventive measure against the disease. In T'ai Chi Ch'uan movement, the neck is erect without pressure. It is centered without inclining to the left or the right. The nose always points to the heart. The movements of the head and neck are integrated and follow smoothly, without any twisting of the neck. These movements from side to side increase the activity of the thyroid gland. The thyroid is also helped by saliva in the mouth. Because saliva comes from the head, Taoists call it "divine water." This secretion contains chemicals that prevent goiter. By placing the tongue against the palate, more saliva lubricates the thyroid gland. Finally, daily massage of the neck can also help prevent goiter and stimulate the thyroid.

THE ADRENAL GLANDS

Located in the kidney area, the adrenal glands regulate many vital body functions. Some adrenal hormones maintain the body's balance of sugar, potassium, sodium, and lesser minerals in the blood. Other hormones constrict blood vessels, thus stimulating the heart and increasing the blood pressure. They also relax respiratory muscles to control asthma and allergies. In addition to combating infection and regulating the body's water content, hormones of the adrenal glands even duplicate those hormones secreted by the testes and ovaries. Fatigue and nervous tension overactivate the adrenals, limiting the body's ability to fight infection and disease.

The adrenal glands are found in the middle part of the central nervous system. This area must be kept very warm in order for the kidneys and glands to function properly. Often when a person becomes old and sick, he cannot produce the necessary warmth and calories. This causes excess water to collect, resulting in such diseases as diabetes. T'ai Chi Ch'uan can help prevent these health disorders. The movements act upon the kidneys to remove wastes. They also activate the adrenals to release more hormones to the systems of the body. The forms concentrate the mind and the *chi* in the abdomen, thus providing the added warmth to evaporate excess water and purify the urine. The heat produced by these exercises also stimulates the testes to increase the production of sperm.

NOTES

1. Chen's *T'ai Chi Ch'uan and Weapons for Self-Defense*, written in Chinese, is considered to be an authoritative text on T'ai Chi Ch'uan. *T'ai Chi Ch'uan: Its Effects and Practical Applications* is the English translation of excerpts from this text (Shanghai, 1940).

2. Books by Y. T. Liu include *The Ancient Chinese Program of Body and Mind Conditioning for All Men and Women Who Hate Exercise* (New York: Magnum Publications, 1970); and *Chinese Martial Arts and T'ai Chi Ch'uan* (New York: Chinese Kung Fu Wu Shu Association, 1971).

3. For further details, see Joseph Needham, *Science and Civilization in China: History of Scientific Thought* (Cambridge: The University Press, 1972), pp. 149–50.

CHAPTER 4:
BREATHING

The concept of breathing has a much broader meaning in China than in the West, for it is understood as including not only the processes of filling the lungs with air and expelling carbon dioxide and other wastes, but also the circulation of the nourishing oxygen to all the tissues of the body through the blood. The word *chi*, which may be translated as "breath," also includes the meanings "vital energy," "vitality," and "spirit." Many of the practices of Taoism, including both meditation and techniques of exercise from the ancient *Tu Na* of Hwang Ti to the T'ai Chi Ch'uan form described later in this book, are designed to improve the circulation of the life-giving *chi* throughout the body and to refine and purify the energy it contains. Some of my other books, including *T'ai Chi Ch'uan and I Ching*,[1] *Taoist Health Exercise Book*,[2] and the forthcoming "T'ai Chi Ch'uan and Meditation," contain detailed discussions of various aspects of breathing and how to develop these Taoist practices. To avoid repetition, I will limit myself here to describing a method that will aid beginners to breathe properly and explaining a few more specialized breathing techniques that can be used to clear the head and other parts of the body, to renew sexual potency, to heal wounds, and cure diseases.

It is possible to inhale as well as exhale through either the mouth or the nose. In general, it is healthier to inhale through the nose, since the tiny hairs in the nostrils filter impurities and dirt from the air that would be absorbed into the lungs if inhaled through the mouth. Also, especially in cold weather, air inhaled through the nose is warmer than that taken through the mouth. On the other hand, exhaling through the mouth makes it possible to expel stale impure air from the body more quickly, and so it is called for in certain practices that will be mentioned below.

The most essential aspect of proper Taoist breathing technique, which must be understood by every beginner, is that the inhaled breath should be taken not only into the lungs, but deep into the abdomen. The point where the breath accumulates is three inches below the navel, and is called the *chi hai* (sea of breath). All the more advanced methods of circulating the *chi* and storing the purified energy require the ability to concentrate the breath in the lower abdominal region, which can be developed through exercise and meditation. Westerners sometimes have difficulty at first in directing the breath down to the abdomen. To some extent, this is because it is customary in the West to expand the chest when inhaling deeply, thus storing the air in the lungs instead. The situation is like that of water flowing downstream toward the sea. If it must first enter a large lake, its momentum will be lost, and it might not reach its final destination. By analogy, if the *chi* is held in the lungs, it cannot reach the "sea of breath." For many beginners, however, the difficulty is not that of getting the right idea, but rather it is due to tensions within the body that prevent them from achieving the correct practice. To help overcome this problem, there are various methods that promote deep breathing and direct the breath from the chest to the abdomen.

One method uses the palms of the hands to guide the

breath. First, place them on the upper abdomen above the navel, like a sash. When breathing out through the mouth, press with the hands to help the abdomen contract and expel the stale air. When breathing in through the nose, relax this pressure gradually and evenly. After practicing this for some time, lower the position of the hands gradually, until they are finally directly over the "sea of breath." Eventually, the breath can be directed there without the aid of the hands, by the will alone.

The success of this method depends to a large extent on the condition and posture of the body. One should practice it with a peaceful mind, and with relaxed muscles. To facilitate this, wear loose clothing and untighten the belt to allow free circulation of blood in the abdomen. Lie face-up on a flat but not too hard surface (such as a carpeted floor or mattress) keeping the head, neck, and spine aligned and straight. Both inhalation and exhalation should be done slowly, gradually, and evenly, without making any sound in the nose or throat. At first, it is best to practice this form of breathing just after getting up in the morning or before going to sleep at night.

After a week or two of practice in the horizontal position, the same breathing exercise can be performed while sitting or standing. By the time it is done in the standing form, it should no longer be necessary to apply pressure on the abdomen with the hands. But it is helpful in performing the standing form to bend forward at the waist to a forty-five-degree angle during each exhalation, returning to a fully erect position during each inhalation. Eventually, one will find it easy to perform this breathing exercise anytime, anywhere, and in any form.

After a long time of practicing regularly, a more advanced stage will be reached, in which the abdomen will feel hot as a result of the powerful energy that accumulates there. At this stage, through proper discipline, it is possible to store this vital energy and also to direct it all over the body—from the brain to the tips of the fingers and to the middle of the soles of the feet (known to Taoists as the "cavities of the bubbling spring") and then back again to the "sea of breath." The recurring cycle of this flow of vital energy through the body has enormous value for the attainment of health and longevity.

Two other kinds of breathing should be mentioned here, for they are described in the Taoist meditation classics, as techniques to be developed in the most advanced stages of the practice of meditation. These are "heel breathing" and "embryo breathing." In heel breathing, the energy originates not in the abdomen alone, but from the heels of feet, affecting the circulation of blood and oxygen throughout the entire body. This form of breathing requires a great deal of careful practice. Embryo breathing is a still more advanced form, which imitates the unborn fetus who absorbs the oxygen directly from its mother, and thus "breathes without breathing." This form of breathing and its significance in meditation are the subject of a detailed treatment in my forthcoming "T'ai Chi Ch'uan and Meditation."

Long before reaching such advanced stages, but after considerable practice of the basic breathing exercise described above, it also becomes possible to take advantage of other more specialized breathing techniques that are particularly beneficial for certain purposes and needs, such as clearing congestion from the head, chest, abdomen, and spine, preventing and curing diseases of the inner organs, increasing sexual potency, protecting oneself in dangerous situations, and even healing others.

The methods of clearing the head, chest, abdomen, and spine require the development of a perception of flow or movement of the *chi* through channels within the body, which is coordinated with the inhaling and exhaling process. At first, great mental concentration is needed to guide the *chi* along the correct path to enable the feeling of flow to develop. After much practice, however, it will happen spontaneously.

For clearing the head, one should concentrate on a movement from the forehead to the crown and then down the back of the head to the medula oblongata at the base of the skull, all while inhaling slowly through the nostrils. Then during exhalation, the mind should concentrate on guiding the *chi* back along the same path: up the back of the head to the crown, then down the forehead to the nose. The practice is most effective when repeated three to five times and is an excellent aid in attaining peace of mind.

For clearing the chest and abdomen, one should begin by exhaling three times through the mouth to expel old air. Then the mind is used to guide the breath down into the region of the stomach and intestines during inhalation and to return it upward and through the nostrils during exhalation. This method should be practiced in a standing position.

A similar method can be used to cleanse the spine and back, but it is much more difficult to learn, and generally requires training from a competent instructor. During inhalation, the *chi* flows down to the abdomen, and from there down to the base of the spinal column, and then up the vertebrae of the spine to the back of the head and up to the crown. During exhalation, it comes down again over the forehead and out through the nostrils. After considerable practice, the direction of the flow can also be reversed, so that it goes up the forehead, down the back of the head and spine, and so on. This cycle can be repeated from three to five times.

Another special breathing technique is called "Six Sounds for the Benefit of the Inner Organs." The six sounds are HA, HU, SHI, SSSSS, SHU, and FU. Each is

particularly beneficial to a specific inner organ and can be
used to cure as well as to prevent ailments that affect it. To
be most effective, the sounds should be pronounced with
strong aspiration while exhaling quickly but not too vio-
lently. For the heart, the sound is HA. For the spleen, it is
HU. SSSSS is for the lungs, SHI is for the solar plexus,
SHU is for the liver, and FU is for the kidneys. To keep
these organs healthy, it is sufficient to practice each sound
a few times each day. If one of the organs is diseased, its
sound should be repeated 36 times in succession while
maintaining a certain posture. Details on the correct procedure for each sound can be found in my *Taoist Health
Exercise Book*.[3]

Another special breathing technique, to be practiced in a
sitting position, has the effect of increasing sexual energy
and potency. For a long time, this technique was a secret
teaching known only to Taoists. In fact, it was traditionally
taught as part of a formal ritual, at which it was necessary
for all to swear an oath not to reveal the procedures. Several reasons may be given to explain this secrecy. For one
thing, sexual practices were not often discussed openly in
traditional Chinese society, lest they be interpreted in a
prurient manner, bringing disgrace to the practitioners.
Furthermore, it was thought that those who were unen-
lightened would be overanxious to attain sexual ecstasy
and might injure themselves by trying to advance too
rapidly in the practice. In addition, there was a superstitious belief that the practice would become less potent if it
were shared with the majority of mankind. Finally, it must
be admitted that maintaining secrecy added an aura of
mystery to those who partook in the clandestine activity.

Another interesting aspect of the traditional practice of
this technique is that it was limited only to men. The description of the breathing method was done with the male
reproductive anatomy in mind, and the benefits of its prac-

tice were seen as increased potency and prevention of premature ejaculation. No thought was given to the possible value of this or other similar practices for women.

I believe that these traditional prejudices are rather out of date today. Many books currently published deal with sexual health and practices quite candidly, and there is no need to be inhibited in discussing information of genuine hygienic value as a result of taboos or superstitions. Furthermore, it is not necessarily true that only men can take advantage of the practice. A similar method can be used by women and has been found to benefit the female reproductive organs and to prevent diseases involving them. Some women have even become able to control their menstrual cycle by practicing a method of this kind.

Here I will describe the technique in such a way that both men and women can practice it. It should be approached with caution and without becoming impatient to improve too quickly, for powerful energy is involved, and physical harm can result from improper use of it.

Begin by sitting on a low chair or on the edge of a bed at knee level, so that the feet rest firmly on the ground. Cover the kneecaps with the open palms of the hands. Inhale through the nose, while bowing forward from the waist to a forty-five-degree angle. At the same time, use mental concentration and the breath to feel a flow of energy from the soles of the feet, up the legs to the genital region. Then exhale through the mouth while gradually straightening at the waist until upright once again, at the same time feeling the energy flow down the legs to the feet. (Note carefully that the coordination of the bending and straightening with the breathing in this exercise is the opposite of that used in the fundamental breathing exercise described earlier in this chapter.) Repeat the cycle of inhalation and exhalation twenty times, feeling the upward and downward flow of energy each time. This should be practiced in the morning just after rising and repeated just before retiring at night. It is best to practice in the open air, but, in cold weather, it will do to sit near a slightly open window.

After three months, a refinement of this technique can be attempted. There is a sensitive point directly between the anus and the genital region. During inhalation, concentrate on drawing the vital energy to this point and from there slowly to the genital region. A man should feel it move toward the tip of the penis; a woman should feel the flow inward toward the uterus.

Another special breathing technique is particularly useful for alleviating fear and overcoming fatigue in the face of imminent physical danger or extreme stress. It should not be practiced regularly, but knowledge of how to use it may be a great help if one should find oneself in a difficult situation. The technique involves becoming taut and unyielding throughout the body very suddenly. The toes dig in, the legs are braced, the anus is tightened, fists and teeth are clenched. The chest is slightly recessed while the shoulders and neck muscles are tensed, so that the spine is straight and rigid. The tongue is placed against the roof of the mouth, the chin drawn back, and the eyes widened. If all this is performed as a single action while at the same time inhaling deeply into the abdomen, it makes the body more powerful, and also arouses courage. One should also be aware, however, that to get hit while the breath is stored inside the body can be dangerous. If one is about to be hit, it is best to inhale sharply through the nose, making the sound "Hnnng!" Then exhale explosively through the mouth with a loud and abrupt "Ha!" This powerful yell may frighten the opponent and build one's own self-confidence. More important, it will release inner tension without damage to one's internal organs, leaving the body relaxed so that the damage from any collision is minimized.

Finally, a word should be said here about the use of the

circulation of the *chi* to heal wounds and illnesses. Through the practice of the fundamental breathing exercise described above, one can develop the ability to circulate the vital energy to any part of the body at will, as well as to store it in the *tan t'ien* region of the abdomen, just above the "sea of breath." If the exercise is performed regularly, the vitality can be stored, like money in a savings bank, until it is needed to relieve pain. If one becomes wounded or ill, the concentration can be used to withdraw it from storage and guide it to the area where it is needed. The really remarkable thing about it is that this energy can be transmitted to others who are in need through the tips of the fingers. Thus the breathing methods described here are not only beneficial to the health of the practitioner but ultimately give him or her the power of healing, which can be used for the benefit of others as well. Some details about how to use it will be given in the chapter on acupressure and massage.

NOTES

1. (New York: Harper and Row, 1972).
2. (New York: Links Books, 1974).
3. *Ibid.*, pp. 61–62.

CHAPTER 5:

HOW TO PERFORM THE T'AI CHI CH'UAN FORM

The T'ai Chi Ch'uan form consists of a series of movements that involve turning, shifting one's weight from one leg to another, bending and unbending the legs, and various arm movements, all coordinated very precisely in a definite sequence. Each of the individual movements has a potential use for self-defense, and some are named after this use. Others are named after the movements of animals that they imitate. The form combines these movements in various different combinations, which comprise its several sections and series.

Traditionally, there have been two distinct T'ai Chi Ch'uan forms. The so-called long form has three sections and includes 108 different movements. The "short form" has two sections and includes thirty-seven movements. The form described in this chapter is intermediate between these. Not as repetitious as the long form, it includes all the important movements, fifty in all, and is divided into two sections. The first section involves seventeen movements. It is easy to learn and to practice, for none of these movements are terribly intricate, but it is the most important part of the form, for it is fundamental to the development of the more advanced parts.

Moreover, to receive the health benefits of T'ai Chi

Ch'uan, it is sufficient to practice the first section. In fact, one can benefit a great deal even by practicing only the first movement of the first section (the beginning of the T'ai Chi Ch'uan form), for the repetition of this movement is nothing less than the practice of standing meditation. The second section of the form is more complicated, and some of the movements that comprise it are individually more difficult. It is more useful for self-defense than the first section, but it can be learned easily only if one is already pretty good at the first section.

To learn to execute the form correctly, it is necessary to practice it slowly and evenly. It should not be thought of as a sequence of discrete postures, but as a continuous smooth process that flows by like water, without any break or pause. The movements should all be done at the same even rate. One should avoid moving suddenly slower or quicker and suddenly more strenuous or more slack. Also, it is best to learn the movements slowly, always concentrating on correct execution. It is much better for health to be able to perform a single movement correctly than to go through many forms that are tense, broken, or otherwise incorrect.

In this description of the movements of the form, I use the directions of the compass (north, south, east, west, and so on) as an aid in explaining the proper orientations of movements. For purposes of the description, it is assumed that in the initial posture, one is facing toward the north. To prevent misunderstanding, however, it should be mentioned that this is done only for convenience, in order to make the description easier to follow (the concepts of right and left, forward and backward, are sometimes confusing, for as soon as one turns, "right" means a different direction). There is no special significance in facing north at the beginning. Some enlightened Taoists are accustomed to begin facing the sun. Actually, any orientation will do just as well, and one should choose orientations so as to make the most comfortable use of the floor space available.

FIRST SECTION

INITIAL POSTURE *(Figure 1)*

Stand erect.

Your mind should be at peace and your body relaxed.

The neck should be straight without tension, so that your head is upright and centered, as if the top of your head were attached by a string to the ceiling.

The eyes look straight forward, open but not too wide.

The nose points down toward the heart.

The mouth is gently closed, the tongue lightly touching the palate. When saliva accumulates, it should be swallowed.

The jaw should be relaxed, and the chin straight.

The shoulders are loose and at the same level, with both arms hanging down naturally.

The chest is flat, neither protruding forward nor sunken in.

The stomach muscles are relaxed, but the abdomen should not stick out unnaturally, bending the spine.

Concentrate the mind on the body's center of gravity, about three inches below the navel. This point is called the *Tan T'ien*, which means "field where the elixir grows." Through mental concentration, the breath should accumulate at this point.

The hands should hang naturally by the sides, with palms facing rear and fingers slightly separated.

The arms are slightly bent at the elbow, so that the elbows are four or five inches away from the body, but the hands are only about one inch away.

The legs should be slightly bent at the knees.

The heels should be together and the toes should point outward, so that the two feet form an angle of 50 to 60 degrees.

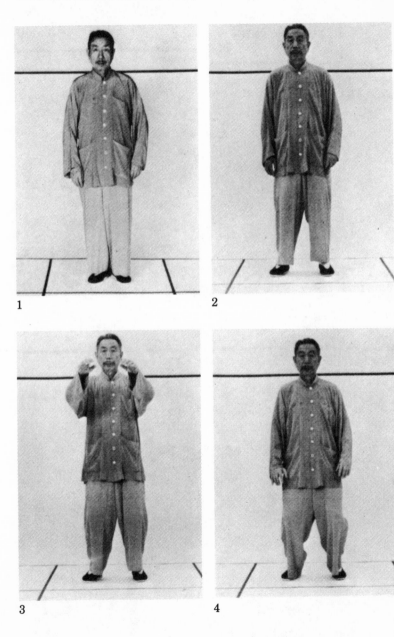

1

2

3

4

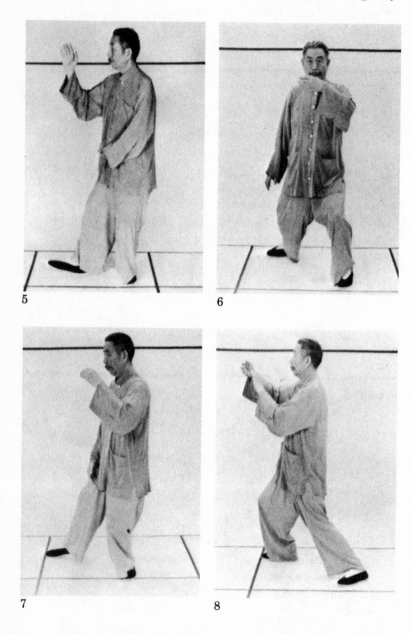

5

6

7

8

BEGINNING OF THE T'AI CHI CH'UAN FORM (*Figures 2, 3, and 4*)

Shift all your weight onto your right foot.

Move your left foot away from the right until the feet are the same distance apart as the width of your shoulders. Put the left foot down so that it points straight forward.

Shifting weight to the left foot, move the right toes inward so that the right foot also points straight forward.

Equalize the distribution of weight between the two feet, which should now be pointing forward, a shoulder-width apart.

Raise both hands forward, keeping them a shoulder-width apart, palms downward, until they are slightly above shoulder level. Simultaneously straighten your legs. During this movement, the elbows stay relaxed, and the hands flow upward as if rising in water.

Drop the hands slightly to the level of the shoulders while drawing them back toward the body. Then press them down to your sides once again, palms downward, simultaneously bending the legs again as at the beginning.

TURN BODY TO RIGHT (*Figure 5*)

Shift weight to the left leg and turn the trunk of the body to the right. While turning, simultaneously:

—raise the right toes two inches off the floor and pivot on the *right* heel until the foot points to the right, perpendicular to the left foot;

—raise the right hand by swinging the arm up from the elbow, so that the elbow, hand, and shoulder form a triangle;

—move the left hand to the front of the body just below the navel, palm facing upward.

GRASP BIRD'S TAIL (LEFT) *(Figure 6)*

The motion of the arms and hands resembles the manner in which one might hold a bird. The left hand is raised upward as if to grasp the bird's neck, while the right slants downward, as if gently to smooth the feathers of his back down to his tail.

Shift your weight to the right foot, allowing it to rest flat on the floor, and turn your body to the left (north), maintaining the hand positions.

During the turn, lift your left heel and pivot on the toes.

Take a big step straight forward with your left foot. As the foot comes down, both feet should be flat on the floor and form an angle of 90 degrees.

Bend your left leg and shift weight onto it until the left leg supports about 80 percent of your weight, the right leg 20 percent.

While shifting the weight, simultaneously:

—raise your left hand from below the navel to chin level, so that it is about a foot and a half from the chin, palm facing inward, and so that the arm is curved gently, the elbow slightly below the level of the hand;

—drop the right arm to your right side;

—turn your waist to the left and pivot on your right heel until the toes move to an angle of 45 degrees.

PUSH UP; WARD OFF; PULL BACK; PRESS FORWARD; PUSH FORWARD; PUSH UP *(Figures 7 and 8)*

Move most of weight onto your left leg and raise your right heel.

Turn your trunk to face east, your right foot pivoting on its toes.

Step straight with your right foot, the toes pointing east.

9

10

11

12

13

14

15

16

As the weight shifts onto your right leg, simultaneously:
—your right hand raises to chin level, the palm facing in;
—your left palm barely touches your right palm;
—your left foot turns inward 45 degrees.

WARD OFF (RIGHT) AND PULL BACK *(Figures 9 and 10)*

The trunk rotates slightly to right (southeast) as your right arm extends and rises with its palm almost facing down. The left hand, following this motion, comes near the right elbow, with its palm facing up toward the right palm.

As you bend your left knee and shift your weight onto your left leg, drop your hands diagonally and downward (northwest), across the body, the palms facing each other.

PRESS FORWARD *(Figures 11 and 12)*

As your left hand circles back and returns past your left ear with the palm facing forward, your right hand rises up to chin level with the palm facing inward.

As the hands move to the front of the body, the left palm lightly touching the right palm, the weight shifts to the right leg and pushes the arms forward (east).

PUSH FORWARD *(Figure 13)*

Separate hands to shoulder width.

Shift weight back to left leg while drawing the hands toward the shoulder, pulling the elbow toward the trunk.

Shift weight on to the right leg, moving east, and push forward both arms slightly bent, palms forward.

TURN BODY AND SINGLE WHIP *(Figures 14, 15, 16, and 17)*

The spiral motion of the left hand as it is extended forward resembles the action of a whip.

Shift weight back and to your left leg, while your arms, with the elbows bent slightly and the palms facing down, are held parallel at shoulder level in front of your body. The toes of your right foot come up, the right foot resting on its heel.

Pivot the trunk over the left leg until your hands, which are still parallel, point northwest. As your trunk pivots, your right foot also pivots on its heel.

Bring the toes of your right foot down and point them north. Shift weight onto your right leg, your trunk facing northwest; simultaneously:

—your left hand moves across the body slightly below waist level, palm up;

—your right arm rotates clockwise at shoulder level. The right arm extends to the right of the body, the fingers pointing down, with all of the fingertips gently touching the tip of the thumb. The elbow points to the floor;

—your left foot pivots on its toes with the heel slightly raised. The toes point northwest.

Take a long and wide step west with the left foot. Then, as the weight shifts onto your left leg, your left arm sweeps up from your chest to press forward with the palm facing down and the fingertips at throat level. Your right foot turns inward 45 degrees until the toes point northwest. The right arm remains at shoulder level with the fingertips still touching the thumb.

PLAY GUITAR (RIGHT) *(Figures 18 and 19)*

With most of the weight still on your left leg, turn your trunk right, until it faces north. At the same time:

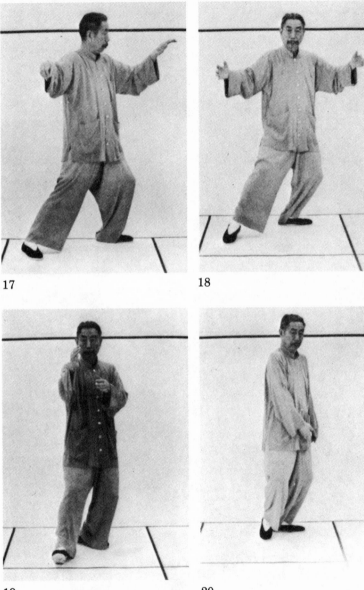

17

18

19

20

21

22

23

24

—your right foot pivots on its toes;

—your arms spread open on the side, hands at shoulder level, the palms facing forward, and elbows relaxed.

From this position your right foot moves leftward until it comes, on its heel, slightly in front of the heel of your left foot. Your right knee is slightly bent.

At the same time, bring your arms together in the front of your trunk, the elbows slightly bent, the palms facing each other. Your right arm is extended at shoulder level with the elbow remaining slightly bent. It is aligned with the right foot, which is also extended. The palm of your left hand is at the same level as your right elbow, about six inches away.

PULL BACK *(Figure 20)*

Keeping weight on left leg, simultaneously:

—your right foot comes on its toes with its heel by your left heel;

—your hands move down toward and alongside the left thigh, the palms facing the thigh.

STEP FORWARD AND STRIKE WITH SHOULDER *(Figure 21)*

Step forward with right foot, toes pointing north; shift weight to right leg, and as the shifting takes place:

—your trunk turns toward the west until your right shoulder points north;

—your left hand moves across to the right until touching lightly your right wrist.

WHITE CRANE SPREADS WINGS *(Figure 22)*

The right hand rises before the forehead, resembling the

wing of a resting crane being spread out. The left foot is
light, and the weight is supported almost entirely on the
right, which also imitates the crane's habit of standing on
one leg while resting.

With the weight on the right leg, simultaneously:

—lift slightly by straightening your right leg, move your
left foot in toward your right foot, and put the toes
down lightly and in line with your right heel;

—your left hand brushes by your left thigh and comes to
the left side of your body, palm back;

—your right hand rises to the right of your forehead, the
elbow is bent, the thumb is toward your right eye, and
the palm faces down.

BRUSH KNEE (LEFT) AND PUSH FORWARD
(Figures 23 and 24)

With the weight still on your right leg, sink slightly by
bending your right knee. As you are sinking, simultaneously:

—your right arm comes down, palm up, beside your right
thigh;

—your left arm moves up, circles across the body, and
comes by the right side of your chest, palm down, facing the right palm.

Step to the west with your left foot, and shift your
weight to it. As the weight shifts:

—your left arm continues circling, coming down and in
front of your body. The hand brushes over your left
knee and comes to the side of your body, palm facing
back;

—your right hand moves up behind the right ear, palm
down, passes by the ear, and continues forward, pointing the fingers toward the west, as if reaching for an
opponent's throat.

PLAY GUITAR (LEFT) *(Figure 25)*

This movement is the mirror image of Play Guitar (Right).

Shift more weight on your left leg and take a small step with your right foot, moving it slightly to the left; your toes come down first and point north.

Shift weight to the right leg as simultaneously:

—your left foot moves in toward the right foot until it comes on its heel. Your left knee is bent slightly in front of the heel of your right foot;

—your left hand is at shoulder level and your left elbow is slightly bent;

—your palms are facing each other;

—your left foot and left hand extend further forward than the right foot and hand;

—your right palm is at the same level as the elbow of your left arm, about six inches away.

BRUSH KNEE FORWARD AND PUSH (LEFT)

This movement essentially repeats that shown in figures 23 and 24.

Your left arm circles down in front of your body and brushes the left knee with its palm as you step west with your left foot. As you shift the weight to your left leg, your right hand passes by your right ear, palm down, and moves forward with the fingertips at throat level.

STEP FORWARD AND PUNCH *(Figures 26, 27, and 28)*

Shift your weight back on your right leg, while at the same time:

—your right hand comes down by your right thigh with the palm facing back;

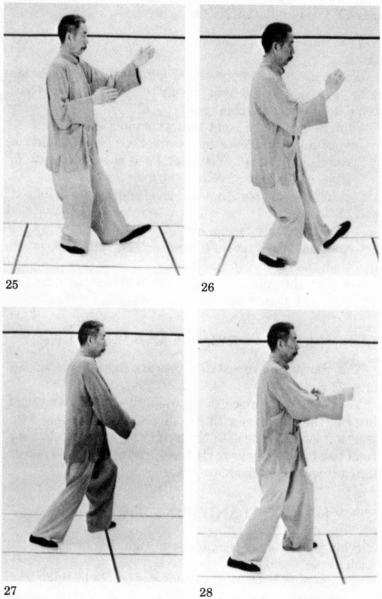

25

26

27

28

—the toes of your left foot come up, the heel remaining on the floor.

Turn the left toes slightly outward, bring them down on the floor, and shift weight onto your left leg.

Step west with your right leg, bringing your foot down with toes pointing northwest.

As the weight shifts onto the right leg, the right arm bends at the elbow, lifting the hand to elbow level. As it comes upward, the hand forms a fist.

Step onto left foot with your toes pointing straight west; your left arm moves across your trunk at chest level.

Shift weight forward onto your left leg. As the weight shifts, your right fisted hand moves punching straight west.

DRAW BACK AND PUSH FORWARD *(Figures 29, 30, and 31)*

Shift the weight back to the right leg, while at the same time:

—your left hand moves under your right elbow, pushing forward and outward with the back of the hand, as it slides under your right forearm.

—pull your right arm back toward the chest while opening your fist.

As the weight continues shifting onto the right leg, the hands separate, moving toward the shoulder, the palms facing west.

Shift the weight forward onto the left leg, pressing west and slightly upward with the arms separated.

CROSS HANDS *(Figures 32, 33, and 34)*

Shift weight back onto your right leg. Simultaneously, facing north:

29

30

31

32

—raise your left toes;

—straighten both arms and raise them almost straight above your head.

Turn trunk until facing north.

During the turn:

—your arms follow the trunk, your right arm circling widely clockwise, your left arm simultaneously circling in the opposite direction.

—your left foot pivots on its heel until the toes point north.

Shift most of the weight on your left leg while your hands continue circling down and up, until they come to a cross at the wrists in front of your chest. The palms are facing the chest with the left palm closer to the chest. Simultaneously:

—move your right foot until it is parallel to and shoulder-width away from your left foot.

—support your weight equally on both legs, and bend your knees slightly.

END OF FIRST SECTION

If you are continuing with the second section of the form, you should omit this movement, going directly from Cross Hands to Bring Tiger to the Mountain. If you are performing only the first section, complete the exercise as follows:

Keeping your knees slightly bent, slowly drop your hands from the crossed position to your sides.

Let your arms come upward in a circular motion and then press them down, while unbending and then bending the legs at the knees, just as in the very first movement of the form.

33

34

35

36

SECOND SECTION

BRING TIGER TO THE MOUNTAIN *(Figures 35 and 36)*

This movement begins the second section and immediately follows the Cross Hands position that ends the first. The crossed hands appear to embrace the tiger, who is then led upward to the mountain with a turn and a step.

With weight on the left leg, turn to the right and take a large step with the right foot in the southeast direction. As your weight shifts onto your right leg, simultaneously:

—your right arm drops, with the hand by the inside of your right knee. The back of the hand pivots over the knee until it hangs on the right side of and slightly above the knee, with the palm facing upward;

—your left arm drops back, and then curves upward, passing by the left ear, the fingertips moving forward at throat level;

—the left foot pivots on its heel until the toes point northeast.

At the conclusion of this movement, the right knee is bent, the left palm faces down with the fingers at ear level and the right palm faces up. Both hands seem to hold a large ball.

PULL BACK; PRESS FORWARD; PUSH FORWARD; TURN BODY; SINGLE WHIP *(Figures 37, 38, 39, 40, 41, 42, 43, and 44)*

This sequence of forms repeats the movements described in the first section. This time, however, they are performed diagonally or along a northwest-southeast line.

In the beginning of the Pull Back form, the hands roll an

37

38

39

40

41

42

43

44

45

46

47

48

imaginary ball in a counterclockwise direction until the left hand is under the ball and the right hand is above it. As your weight shifts onto your left leg, the arms come down by the left side of your body as in the earlier Pull Back form.

FIST UNDER ELBOW *(Figures 45, 46, 47, and 48)*

Shift weight back to your right leg. As you step westward with your left leg (toes pointing southwest) your left arm swings horizontally at shoulder level, toward the left, the palm of the hand facing down. The movement of the arm is coordinated with that of the left leg.

Shift weight to your left leg, and take a half-step with the right foot, in a westward direction (toes pointing northwest). At the same time:

—your right hand, with its palm facing upward, swings horizontally at shoulder level toward the left.

—your left arm curves down to the side of your body.

Shift your weight again to your right leg, bend the right knee, and simultaneously:

—move your left leg, the foot resting on its heel, to the right, with the toes pointing westward and up.

—bring your left arm up, above your left leg. The arm is bent at the elbow, which is pointing down to your knee and forming a 45-degree angle; the hand is at chin level with the palm facing north.

—move your right arm across the front of your body, and make a fist with your right hand under your left elbow.

STEP BACK AND REPULSE MONKEY (RIGHT) *(Figures 49 and 50)*

This movement is very useful for self-defense in a situation that involves retreat. As one steps back, the right hand holds the monkey's arm while the left hand strikes his face. The front foot is light, supporting very little weight, so that it is ready either to kick or to step back.

As your right arm drops slowly by the right side of your body, the palm faces forward (westward) and slightly upward; simultaneously:

—extend the left arm forward (westward) while your forearm turns, until the palm faces forward and slightly downward, the fingertips pointing forward.

Turn the trunk of your body to the right, while at the same time:

—your right arm circles back and upward, palm up, until the hand reaches shoulder level;

—your left arm comes down to shoulder level; turn the forearm until the palm of your left hand also faces up.

Both hands should now be at shoulder level with the palms facing upward.

Turn your trunk forward to face west, and step back with your left leg; simultaneously:

—your right arm comes up, passes by the right ear with the fingertips pressing forward at the level of your eyes. The elbow is slightly bent;

—your left arm falls slowly down by the left side of your body, the palm facing west and slightly upward.

—the left foot steps back, toes first. Gradually shift your weight to the left leg while pointing the toes of your right foot westward. The sole of your right foot is resting lightly on the floor.

STEP BACK AND REPULSE MONKEY (LEFT)

Turn your trunk to the left, while at the same time:

—your left arm circles back and upward, palm up, until the hand reaches shoulder level;

—your right arm comes down to shoulder level, turning

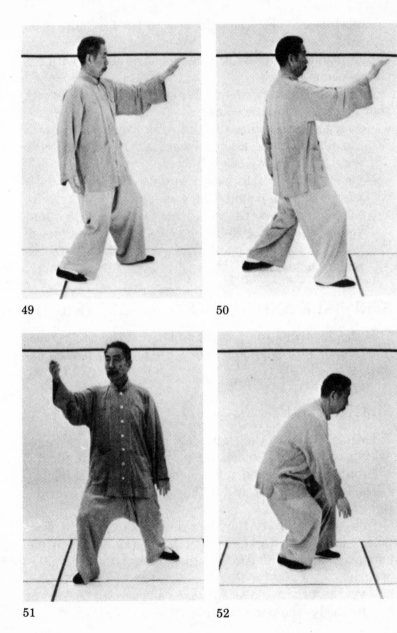

49

50

51

52

the forearm until the palm of your left hand also faces up.

Both hands should be at shoulder level again, with the palms facing upward.

Turn your trunk forward to face west, and step back with your right leg; simultaneously:

—your left arm comes up, passes by your left ear with the fingertips pressing forward at the level of your eyes. The elbow is slightly bent;

—your right arm falls slowly down by the right side of your body, the palm facing west and slightly upward;

—the right foot steps back, toes first. Gradually shift your weight to the right leg while pointing the toes of your left foot westward. The sole of your left foot is resting lightly on the floor.

STEP BACK AND REPULSE MONKEY (RIGHT)

Turn your trunk to the right and repeat the circling motion of your arm, stepping back with your left foot as described previously.

SLANT FLYING *(Figure 51)*

The movement of the right hand slanting upward diagonally to the right resembles the pattern of a bird in flight.

Drop your right hand across and over the left thigh.

The left hand circles up and then down, crossing over the right hand.

Turn your trunk to the right and, with the right foot, take a large step to the right (135-degree angle) in the northeast direction. As you turn your trunk, simultaneously:

—your right arm moves up diagonally across the front of the body, the palm slanting up at temple level;

—your weight shifts onto the right leg while your left foot pivots on its heel until the toes point northwest;

—the left arm drops to the side, the left hand brushing across the left knee.

PLAY GUITAR (RIGHT)

With most of your weight on the right leg, adjust your left foot by moving its toes slightly outward (northwest) with the heel pivoting on the floor.

Shift your weight onto the left leg and repeat the movement as described in the first section.

PULL BACK; STEP FORWARD AND STRIKE WITH SHOULDER

Repeat the movement as described in the first section.

WHITE CRANE SPREADS WINGS

Repeat the movement as described in the first section.

BRUSH KNEE (LEFT) AND PUSH FORWARD

Repeat the movement as described in the first section.

NEEDLE AT SEA BOTTOM *(Figure 52)*

The region just below the navel where the breath accumulates is called the "sea of breath." In this movement, the hands descend below this sea to the area between the two knees. The right hand stretches naturally, resembling a needle. The left hand resting gently on the right wrist seems to hold onto the needle.

Shift weight to your left leg and take a small adjustment

step to your left (southward) with the right foot. The heel of your right foot should be almost behind your left heel, and your right toes should now point in the northwest direction.

Shift weight onto your right leg and, as you bend your right leg, lowering and sinking the body, simultaneously:

—place the left foot on its toes about eight inches in front of the right heel, the toes pointing westward.

—straighten and lower the right arm, the palm of the right hand facing southward.

—follow this downward motion with the left hand, which is placed over the right wrist as it is lowered.

As your body continues sinking down, drop both hands down by your right knee, the left hand still lightly touching your right wrist.

PLAY ARMS LIKE A FAN *(Figure 53)*

The two arms separate, resembling the opening of a Chinese folding fan.

Lift body and step forward (westward) and to the side with the left foot, the toes pointing straight west. As you lift your body, and as your weight shifts onto the bent left leg, the hands are spread like the two sides of a Chinese folding fan. At the same time:

—your trunk turns slightly right (northwest);

—your left arm moves in a forward arc, the palm facing west and the fingertip as if striking the solar plexus of an opponent.

—the back of your right hand comes slightly above and behind your right ear, the palm facing westward and slightly upward.

TURN BODY AND STRIKE FIST TO BACK
(Figure 54)

Shift weight onto your right leg; turn your trunk to the right until it faces north, your right elbow pointing east. As your trunk is turning, simultaneously:
— your left foot pivots on its heel until its toes point northward;
— your right hand forms a fist and your right forearm moves out to the side of your body (eastward), the back of your hand facing east (as if striking the top of an opponent's head);
— your left arm drops by the side of your body.

STEP FORWARD AND PUNCH *(Figure 55)*

Shift weight to your left leg while your right arm comes down by the side of your body.

Pivot your right foot on its heel until its toes point southeast, while your right fist comes up and swings to the right, at waist level.

Step eastward with the left foot, and simultaneously:
— punch with your right fist;
— bring your left hand above the middle part of your right forearm, which is moving eastward.

HIT TIGER (LEFT) *(Figures 56 and 57)*

The two fists appear to hit the tiger in two places at once. The upper lands on the side of his head, while the lower finds his ribs.

Circle upward and outward with your right arm and open your fist so that your right palm faces down. At the same time, turn your left palm upward.

Step back with your left leg, placing your foot so that the toes point northeast.

53

54

55

56

57

58

59

60

Shift your weight onto the left leg, while at the same time turning your body to the left, and drop your arms diagonally downward in front of your body with your right foot flat on the floor, toes pointing southeast.

Shift the weight to the right leg, and step forward with your left foot, so that the toes point directly east. At the same time, bring both arms upward in a circular, clockwise motion, with open palms facing east. As the arms circle, the hands form fists and weight gradually shifts to the left (forward) leg. The fists stop so that the left hits the temple, while the right hits the lower ribs of an imaginary opponent.

HIT TIGER (RIGHT) *(Figures 58 and 59)*

This movement repeats the previous one, but in the opposite direction. The only difference is that as the weight shifts to the rear (right) leg, the left foot must turn outward, pivoting on the heel, until the toes point to the northeast.

KICK WITH TOES *(Figure 60)*

Open the fists and circle the arms down and outward. As your arms continue the circling movement:
—draw your right foot back and touch the floor slightly with the toes;
—cross the hands at the wrists, in front of your chest. Both palms are facing your chest, the left palm being closer to the chest.

With the hands still crossed in front of your chest, rotate your forearms until both palms face away from your chest (east).

As you spread your arms with the hands at shoulder level, the elbows are slightly bent, and the palms are still facing forward:

—lift your right leg and kick forward (east) and upward;
the thigh is horizontal and the knee is bent, forming a
135-degree angle;

As your right foot relaxes back, the thigh still horizontal,
the knee forms a 90-degree angle, and the toes come pointing down;

—both hands form fists, move inward, and brush the
knuckles down on either side of the bent knee.

HIT OPPONENT'S EARS WITH FISTS
(Figures 61 and 62)

As you step forward (eastward) with the right foot:
—the arms continue downward and outward.

Shift weight onto the right leg and simultaneously:
—move the arms upward and toward the center in front
of your face, at ear level.

TURN BODY AND KICK *(Figures 63 and 64)*

Shift weight onto your left leg and turn your trunk to the
left to face north, while at the same time:
—pivot your right foot on its heel until the toes point
north.
—relax fists and circle hands downward and outward.

As your hands continue the circling motion and start
coming upward until the wrists cross at chest level:
—shift weight onto your right leg.
—pivot the left foot on its toes until they point northwest.

At the end of this movement, the palms are turned toward the chest, the left palm being closer to the chest, and
the fingertips of both hands are almost touching the shoulders.

As you turn the trunk further to the left (facing northwest):

61

62

63

64

—kick upward and westward with the left heel.

—move your left hand westward, above the knee, with the palm slightly down.

—move your right hand up to protect the right temple, the palm facing northwest and slightly down.

BRUSH KNEE FORWARD AND PUSH (LEFT)

Step westward with the left foot, toes pointing west; brush knee with the left hand, and push forward with the right hand.

This is a repeat of the movement described in the first section.

WAVE HANDS LIKE CLOUDS (RIGHT)
(Figures 65, 66, and 67)

With weight on the left leg, pivot the left foot on its heel toward the right, until the toes point north.

As your trunk turns to the right, simultaneously:

—shift weight onto the right leg.

—pivot the left foot on its heel and point the toes north.

While you continue turning the trunk to the right, the arms follow the turn very lightly:

—the left hand moves across the front of the lower part of the trunk, palm up.

—the right hand is drawn to shoulder level; the palm is down, the forearm is slanted, and the elbow is pointed toward the ground.

Bring your left foot forward (north) in line with, and parallel to, your right foot; the distance between your feet should be slightly greater than the width of your shoulders. Your weight should be still on your right leg.

When your trunk is turned to the right as far as possible:

—turn your right forearm outward; the palm of your

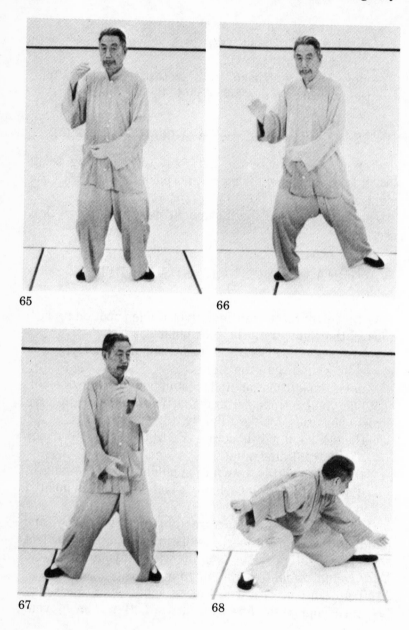

65

66

67

68

right hand faces east, and your fingertips point in the same direction.

The body turns left from the waist as the weight moves to the left. Simultaneously the arms exchange:

—the right arm moves down across the lower trunk, palms up;

—the left arm moves up and across to the left as the body turns.

Alternating from right to left, this movement is performed three times.

Repeat the movement Single Whip as described in the first section.

SNAKE CREEPS DOWN *(Figure 68)*

With the weight on the left leg, pivot your right foot on its heel until the toes point north.

Shift weight onto the right leg.

Lower your body over your right heel until you are almost sitting on it. At the same time:

—your left foot pivots inward on its heel until the toes point northwest.

—your right arm remains in the Single Whip position (with the fingers touching the thumb, but straightened at the elbow).

—your left hand moves down, passing by the inside of the lower thigh and continuing down past the calf.

As your left hand continues to move alongside the left calf, begin an upward sweep and:

—turn the left toes forward (westward).

—shift your weight forward onto the left leg, which is bent.

Straighten the left leg to lift your body, while at the same time:

—your left arm continues its upward movement, the palm facing north.

—your right foot pivots on its heel until the toes point northwest.

—your right arm comes down by the right side of your body.

GOLDEN COCK ON ONE LEG (RIGHT)
(Figures 69 and 70)

Move the right arm and right knee upward together into a striking position. Simultaneously:

—the right arm moves up, forming an acute angle at the elbow; the hand is at the level of the nose; the palm faces south.

—the right knee rises, forming a right angle; the thigh is horizontal; the toes are pointing down, the knee points west.

—the left arm drops by the left side of the body.

GOLDEN COCK ON ONE LEG (LEFT) *(Figure 71)*

Step back with right foot, toes pointing northwest, and shift weight onto right leg. Your right elbow remains bent and your right hand is at shoulder height and the toes of your left foot come off the ground.

Follow the description given for the previous movement, reversing the sides.

HIGH PAT ON HORSE (RIGHT) *(Figure 72)*

One hand appears to move upward to pat the horse's back while the other grasps the reins.

Step back with the left foot, the toes pointing westward; and then shift your weight onto your left leg, while at the same time:

69

70

71

72

—your left elbow comes against the left side of your trunk, by the waist. The left hand is at waist level, the fingertips are pointing northwest and the palm is facing up;

—your right hand, with the palm facing down, moves slightly above the left palm and back across your left forearm.

Shift your weight onto your right leg, simultaneously moving your trunk and arms diagonally, in the northwest direction, with the hand moving upward. At the same time:

—your right hand, with the palm still facing down, slides above the palm of your left hand and reaches the height of your throat. Your right elbow is slightly bent;

—your left hand, with the palm still facing up, reaches chest height, in line with your right elbow.

SEPARATE FEET AND KICK (RIGHT)
(Figure 73)

Shift the weight back onto your left leg, and let both hands drop back and down along the left side of your trunk. Then, with the weight still on the left:

—your left arm moves up and around until the left hand comes to chin height, with the palm turned away from your face;

—your right hand moves up until its wrist crosses with the wrist of the left hand; the right wrist is in front of the left wrist. The palm of the right hand also faces outward.

Kick in the northwest direction with the right toes at shin level, keeping the sole parallel to the floor. At the same time:

—your right forearm slides forward (northwest) above your kicking right leg; the right hand is now at chest level with the palm facing southwest;

—your left hand slides up to temple height, slightly behind your left ear with the palm facing west.

HIGH PAT ON HORSE (LEFT) *(Figure 74)*

This movement is the mirror image of High Pat on Horse (Right). It is done in exactly the same way, except that left and right are reversed.

SEPARATE FEET AND KICK (LEFT)

This movement is the mirror image of Separate Feet and Kick (Right). It is done in exactly the same way, except that left and right are reversed.

TURN BODY AND KICK *(Figures 75, 76, and 77)*

Move your left heel up beside your upper inner right calf, so that your left knee points southwest. At the same time:
—your left arm moves to the right across your trunk, the left palm facing your body and slightly below waist level.
—your right forearm is extended out (north) and down, the hand slightly above waist level, with open palm facing west.

Swing your right arm to the left in a wide circling motion, propelling your body to the left and around in a full half turn until your trunk and right toes face southeast; your left knee points east. Kick southward with the left heel at waist height, while at the same time:
—your right hand moves up to protect the right temple, the palm facing south;
—your left forearm strikes eastward, the palm open and facing south, the elbow almost touching the left thigh.

BRUSH KNEE AND PUSH (LEFT)

Repeat the movement as described in the first section.

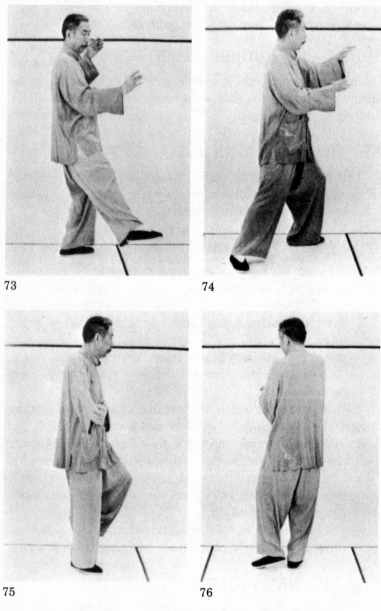

73

74

75

76

77

78

79

80

BRUSH KNEE AND PUSH (RIGHT) *(Figure 78)*

Shift weight back onto your right leg, while at the same time:
—your left foot pivots outward on its heel, the toes pointing up and northeast;
—your left arm comes across your trunk, the palm facing up and slightly below waist level;
—your right forearm is across the trunk at shoulder level, the right palm facing the left palm as if holding a large ball.

Shift weight onto the left leg and step east with your right foot (heel first), the toes pointing eastward. Then, as you shift weight onto the right leg:
—your left arm circles back, around and up. Your left hand then passes by the left ear and moves forward (east) with the fingertips at throat level.
—your right hand brushes across the right knee.

STEP FORWARD AND PUNCH TO OPPONENT'S LOWER ABDOMEN *(Figure 79)*

As you shift your weight back onto your left leg:
—your left arm lowers by the left side of your body, the palm of the hand facing forward.
—your right hand follows the motion of the left hand, the right palm turned toward the left palm.
—your right foot pivots on its heel, the toes turning slightly outward (southeast) and up.

As you shift your weight onto your right leg, your trunk rotates to the right. Both arms widely sweep to the right, the hands at navel level, and the palms facing downward.

With your left foot, step forward (eastward) with the toes pointing east, and, simultaneously:
—shift weight onto the left leg.
—your left hand brushes your left knee.

—your right fist punches forward to opponent's lower abdomen.

STEP FORWARD

Shift your weight back onto your right leg, while:
—both hands, palms facing each other, come along the right side of your body.
—your left foot pivots on its heel, the toes pointing slightly out (northeast).
Step forward and slightly to the right (eastward) with the right foot, the toes pointing east.

Repeat the movements Push Up; Ward Off; Pull Back; Press Forward; Push Forward; Turn Body and Single Whip, as described in the first section.

FAIR LADY WORKS AT SHUTTLE (LEFT)
(Figures 80 and 81)

This movement should be performed so lightly and gracefully that it resembles those of a fair young lady. The motion of the hands to the left and right is like that of a shuttle as it moves back and forth.

Shift weight backward onto your right leg and turn your trunk to the right as far as possible, while simultaneously:
—your left foot pivots on its heel as far right as possible;
—your left hand comes across your trunk slightly below waist level, with the palm facing upward.
—your right hand opens up and comes in front of your chin, the palm facing down.

As your trunk continues the rotation to the right until it faces northeast:
—your weight shifts onto your left leg;
—your right foot pivots on its toes, the heel moving slightly to the left;
—your right arm moves slightly down toward your left arm.

81

82

83

84

Shift weight onto your right leg and then step northeast with your left foot, the toes pointing in the same direction. Then shift your weight onto the left leg, while at the same time:

—your left hand moves up to eyebrow level, the palm faces forward and is slightly slanted toward the ground;

—your right fingertips press forward straight ahead (northeast) at the level of the solar plexus.

FAIR LADY WORKS AT SHUTTLE (RIGHT)
(Figures 82, 83, 84, 85, and 86)

Shift weight backward onto your right leg and turn your trunk to the right as far as possible, while simultaneously:

—your left foot pivots on its heel until the toes point southeast;

—your right hand comes across your trunk, slightly below waist level, with the palm facing upward;

—your left hand moves slightly down at chin level, the palm facing down.

Shift weight onto your left leg and, as your trunk continues the rotation to the right, take a big step with your right foot, making a three-quarter (135-degree) turn, so that the toes point to the northwest.

Shift your weight onto your right leg, while simultaneously:

—your right hand moves up to eyebrow level; the palm faces forward and is slightly slanted toward the ground;

—your left fingertips press forward straight ahead (northwest) at the level of the solar plexus;

—your left foot pivots on its heel until the toes point westward.

85

86

87

88

FAIR LADY WORKS AT SHUTTLE (LEFT)

Shift weight backward onto your left leg and take a small step toward the west, with your right foot, the toes pointing in that direction, while moving your right hand down to waist level.

Shift weight onto your right leg and continue the movement as previously described.

FAIR LADY WORKS AT SHUTTLE (RIGHT)

Repeat the movement as previously described. The only difference is that now you will be facing in the opposite direction.

Repeat the movements: Grasp Bird's Tail (Left); Push Up; Ward Off; Pull Back; Press Forward; Push Forward; Turn Body; Single Whip, as described. Then repeat Snake Creeps Down, as also described previously.

STEP FORWARD, SEVEN STARS *(Figure 87)*

The crossed hands in this movement resemble the configuration of a group of seven stars in the sky surrounding the North Star.

As your body rises up, turn your right toes in, and center your weight onto your left leg. At the same time:

—your hands form fists and cross at the wrists in front of the upper part of your chest; the left wrist is closer to the chest, behind the right wrist; the knuckles face forward (westward);

—your right foot moves on its toes directly in front of your left heel.

RIDE TIGER TO THE MOUNTAIN *(Figure 88)*

This movement involves sitting back and bending the

legs, as if astride the back of a (tame) tiger. The right hand extending upward appears to hold a whip, as if to goad the tiger to run faster.

Step back with your right foot, the toes pointing to the northwest and shift your weight onto your right leg, at the same time dropping both arms to the side of your body, brushing both thighs with the fingertips.

Circle your right hand back, to the side, and up to temple level. The palm is slightly slanted down and is facing northwest; the elbow forms a 90-degree angle. At the same time, your left foot slides back onto its toes and comes in front of your right heel, the toes pointing westward.

Note: This movement is similar to White Crane Spreads Wings, described in the first section. The main difference is that here the right hand circles back and to the side before coming up beside the head, whereas in the White Crane, it is raised directly upward from the front of the thigh. A more subtle difference is that the right leg, supporting the weight, is kept more bent in this movement than in the White Crane, in which it is straightened slightly.

TURN BODY AND DO LOTUS KICK
(Figures 89, 90, and 91)

The full 360-degree turn in this movement imitates the round leaves of the lotus plant, while the leg kick from left to right is like the wind blowing the lotus.

Drop right arm diagonally across body to left as far as it will go, without forcing, so that the palm faces east. At the same time, turn your left hand to face forward, moving the left arm forward slightly, and rotate the forearm to the left and slightly out until the palm faces the west.

Lift your left foot off the ground, slightly forward, and turn your body to the right, making a full turn (360 degrees) on the ball of the right foot; this is accomplished by

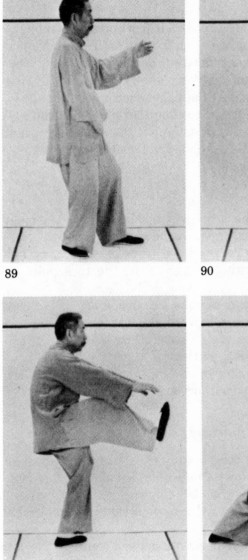

89

90

91

92

swinging the left leg and both arms (palms facing down) to the right.

Finish the turn and, as your left foot comes down on the ground, toes pointing west, shift your entire weight onto your left leg, the knee. bending deeply; your right toes lightly touch the floor, and your arms rise in front of your trunk at shoulder height, the palms facing downward.

Lift your right leg in a circling movement (clockwise), touching, with the toes, first the left then the right palm, while the arms remain extended in front of your chest.

SHOOT TIGER *(Figure 92)*

The position of the arms and hands in this movement resembles those of an archer as he shoots an arrow.

As your right leg comes down from the kick, step forward (westward) with the right foot, the toes pointing west. As you step:
—your hands form fists, knuckles facing up;
—your left fist moves forward at chest level;
—your right fist moves forward at ear level;
—your left toes point southwest.

Shift your trunk and weight forward onto your right leg and simultaneously punch forward with both fists.

CIRCLE FIST *(Figure 93)*

Shift your weight back onto your left leg, and let your arms circle out and down to the side, opening up the fists. The left arm stops by your left thigh.

Shift your weight forward onto your right leg and simultaneously:
—make a fist with your right hand and continue the circling movement clockwise to hit an imaginary opponent's head;

93

—move your left arm across your trunk at stomach level, the palm facing the body.

Now complete the form by repeating the movements: Step Forward and Punch; Draw Back; Push Forward; Cross Hands; and End, as described at the end of the first section.

CHAPTER 6:

ADDITIONAL EXERCISE TECHNIQUES OF THE TAOIST TRADITION

The T'ai Chi Ch'uan form described in the previous chapter is an ideal health exercise for those who can learn it. If it is practiced as much as an hour every day, good health will almost surely result. Nevertheless, it is only one of many different variations of gymnastic techniques for health and longevity that have been developed over the centuries in China. Many of these techniques seem to have originated in the observations of animal movements. Chuang Tzu, for example, mentions stretching the neck like a bird for longevity. The third-century physician Hwa T'o designed a series of five health exercises whose movements resemble those of the tiger, the bear, the monkey, the deer, and the bird. Even Chang San Feng, who developed T'ai Chi Ch'uan during the Sung dynasty, was influenced by having witnessed a fight between a crane and a snake.

Among the various traditional exercises, several are very simple and, though based on the same principles as the T'ai Chi Ch'uan form, are much easier to learn. These can be practiced daily by almost anyone, even the very old or partially infirm. They have the same general effects on health as the more elaborate form and can be used as a preparation for learning T'ai Chi by those who do not feel

108

ready to begin it or who do not have access to a good T'ai Chi Ch'uan teacher.

In this chapter, we will describe three simple types of exercise: a simple standing form with four variations, the method of swinging arms, and the ancient "Eight Pieces of Treasure." At the end of the chapter we will briefly mention a more advanced method of Taoism—the practice of sitting meditation.

A SIMPLE STANDING FORM

There are four variations of the standing form, but all four share some common attributes. For example, in all four the feet are at shoulder width, with the toes pointed in 45 degrees toward each other. The body's weight is on the "full" leg. The palms of the hands are open, the fingers naturally curved. The mind and the *chi* (breathing) are directed to the abdomen, which is slightly contracted. The chest is held forward but flat—rather than expanded— with support from raised shoulders and an erect spine. The eyes focus on the tip of the nose. Breathing is even, steady, full, quiet. The ears listen to the breathing, implying still-ness, composure, and relaxed concentration.

The first standing form adopts this position, with the arms hanging naturally at the sides of the body. The breathing in this form differs from that used in the three standing exercises that follow. In this instance, place the tongue against the roof of the mouth when inhaling through the nose; hold the *chi* in the abdomen; then lay the tip of the tongue along the bottom of the front lower teeth and exhale stale air through the mouth. In subsequent forms, the tongue remains poised against the palate, and each unit of breathing is performed only through the nose.

The second form generally retains the same posture as the first. This time, however, the arms extend at shoulder width in front of the body—parallel to the ground like those of a somnambulist. The tips of the fingers point up, so that the open palms appear to be protecting the face. Inhale and exhale through the nose between ten and twelve times.

The third form resembles a cross, with the arms extended at shoulder height at either side of the body rather than in front of it. As before, the palms are open, the fingers pointing up, and no more than a dozen units of breathing are completed.

The last of the four standing forms positions the arms down and back, the open palms facing away from the body. The practitioner's posture resembles that of a person braced against a flat wall or holding back a crowd. Breathe through the nose as before.

In all standing forms, one inhale and one exhale count as a unit. Depending on physical condition, the beginner should attempt no more than ten or twelve units with any given form. After about a month, the number of units can be increased by three. The four variations of standing exercise can be practiced interchangeably. However, no good will come of them unless they are performed regularly on a daily basis for an extended length of time.

The sitting form of this exercise requires a location that is flat, provides firm support, and is protected from dampness, chill, or noise. A floor, a bed, or some areas of ground outdoors will do. Sit up with both legs extended in front of you. The knees should be locked, but beginners should not force this position until they have gradually and safely mastered it. The feet point up, with the toes inclined a bit toward each other.

With open palms facing the ground, sit on your hands. Slightly lean forward with your head—not with the shoulders—while keeping the spinal cord straight. Pull in the muscles of the diaphragm. As with the standing forms, keep the mouth closed and the surface of the tongue resting against the palate. Listen in relaxed concentration to your own nasal breathing, while your eyes focus centerward. Hold the *chi* and the mind in the abdomen for fifty to a hundred units of breathing. The number depends upon the physical condition of the practitioner, the degree of familiarity with the exercise, and the amount of time available.

The reclining form resembles the sitting in most respects, except that the body lies prone with a small pillow supporting the base of the skull. Breathing through the nose is performed from fifty to a hundred times, subject to the aforementioned considerations.

The standing exercise is most effective when it is performed in the open air among foliage in a quiet setting. If the air becomes damp with foggy mists or rain, or if the calm is disturbed by noise or gusting winds, come inside at once. Standing exercise is best performed in the morning, shortly after waking; reclining exercise is best in the evening hours, before going to sleep; sitting exercise can be performed any time.

There are exceptions. Persons should refrain from these exercises until at least twenty minutes after eating. Pregnant women and people ill with fever or internal hemorrhages must not even attempt the forms.

Otherwise, wear loose clothing when preparing to do the forms. Do not let yourself be distracted by random thoughts or the radio or telephone. This is not a time for conversing with others, since mind, breathing, and movement ought to combine into a whole. If you are interrupted during the middle of a form, do not pick up where you have left off: start over.

Beginners will be surprised by the various changes in their bodies as they perform these exercises. Do not be upset by unusual amounts of warmth and perspiration or by belches or breaking wind. These symptoms indicate that the body is responding well to the exercise. Nor should you be afraid if your hands feel numb, limbs seem sore, or arms tremble. Within a few months this physical discomfort will subside, and, coincidentally, the mouth will begin producing more saliva.

When you have completed the exercise, your body should feel very warm. At this time, it is most inadvisable to take cold refreshment. Wait at least five or ten minutes for the body's temperature to cool naturally. If this series of exercises has led the body to perspire, towel yourself dry at once to protect yourself from illness.

All three forms of the exercise benefit the body. They help the weak to gain physical strength with which to stave off disease. And those already strong will experience an increase in energy, mental uplift, and sound sleep. If continued daily, the exercises will prolong youth.

The forms heal and prevent disease in many parts of the body. In the stomach area, they check indigestion, constipation, and bleeding in the intestines. Conditions involving weak kidneys, nocturnal emission, inflammation of the womb, and menstrual complications may also be improved. Furthermore, performing these exercises regularly can help cure insomnia, rheumatism, high or low blood pressure, backache, asthma, tuberculosis, and polio.

Clearly, standing, sitting, and reclining exercises can help you achieve better breathing habits and some peace of mind. But their combination of Tao Yin (breathing exercises) and T'u Na (gentle calisthenics) provides an approach to improved health and longevity as well, in a series of movements that are uncomplicated, easy to perform, and not overly strenuous, even for older persons.

Finally, here is an exercise for hands and feet together. Balance on your left leg. Raise the right foot five inches off the ground and raise your left hand to ear level. Shake your left hand and right foot vigorously. Then change hands and feet, balance on your right leg, and repeat. This simple exercise will reduce fatigue and tension. It is also effective as an immediate cure for leg cramps during the night. Just do this exercise, shaking the cramped leg, and the cramp will release.

SWINGING ARMS

Recently, "Swinging Arms," a simple health exercise, has become popular in both the People's Republic of China and Nationalist China. Not as complicated as many forms of yoga, this exercise requires no training or undue exertion. It can be performed at any time, in any place, in a limited amount of space, and without special equipment. For this reason, it is of special benefit to the office worker who is sedentary and restricted to a small area of space. Regardless of sex or age, the exercise can be performed regularly and with ease. It is especially accessible to the elderly.

Swinging Arms promises many physical benefits: to relax the joints, lower high blood pressure, increase energy, help digestion, promote a peaceful mind, and, by increasing body activity, stimulate blood circulation. Creating more body heat helps the body digest food, displace wastes, and create energy. Its upward and downward movements of the diaphragm vibrate the stomach and both of the intestines. Indirectly, appetite is improved, as the body receives more nourishment and calories from ingested food. The kidneys and liver also benefit from this vibrating motion. In addition to helping the circulation and digestion, the exercise is said to cure piles and rheumatism.

In China it is claimed that Swinging Arms is an effective treatment against cancer. Many Chinese physicians believe that cancer is caused by bad circulation. When the *chi* cannot flow sufficiently through the blood, stagnation occurs and wastes accumulate in the body tissues. The lymph nodes, which remove wastes from the blood, cannot function properly, so that the wastes become toxic. Swinging Arms improves the circulation, resulting in the excretion of wastes and in improved health.

In many respects, Swinging Arms resembles T'ai Chi Ch'uan. The feet are firmly placed flat on the ground, at shoulder width. The body's weight is placed not in the shoulders but in the legs. The trunk of the body is straight, with the center of gravity at the waist. There is no tension in the groin area, the abdomen does not protrude, and the chest is not inflated. The spinal column is straight and erect. The neck and head, too, are erect but relaxed. The mouth is naturally closed, not tense. The eyes look forward, focusing on a point in space. The mind concentrates without thinking. The energy of the *chi* and the mind are directed to the abdomen, or *tan t'ien*, and the body sinks its weight into the legs and feet. This is very similar to the beginning posture of T'ai Chi Ch'uan.

The main action of the exercise takes place in the arms and hands. At the start, the arms should hang naturally at the sides of the body. Fingers of the hands should retain their natural curve, neither joined nor separated too much. With the palms of both hands facing forward, bring both arms forward and upward to about shoulder level. The swinging motion should be light and effortless: From the navel up the body should be light, as 80 percent of its weight resides in the legs. Now swing the arms back down at either side, thrusting with a smooth and even force. Consider this one completed swing.

The swinging motion should be continued at a regular and easy rate until you feel tired or strained. Do not foolishly believe that you will get quicker results if you perform the exercise more rapidly. Do as many swings as your physique and age permit without fatigue. You can increase the number of swings as your body grows stronger. Gradually, you should be able to complete three hundred or even a thousand.

When you first begin doing the exercise, you may become distressed by the results. The body will burp and break wind, because you are relaxed and a vibrating action on the stomach and intestines is aiding the digestive system. The legs and feet will feel sore and swollen, because the *chi* and fresh blood are filling the lower extremities. Increased circulation also causes the body to perspire more. As the physical condition of the body improves with continued practice of swinging arms, however, these problems go away.

EIGHT PIECES OF TREASURE

From the time of the Yellow Emperor—around 2000 B.C.—those who practice Chinese exercise (and even boxers) have been familiar with the "Eight Pieces of Treasure."[1] These exercises are so named because there are eight movements in all, coordinated with the eight *I Ching* trigrams of the Pa Kua exercises.[2] Whereas other exercises move the outer limbs and are called external movements, the Eight Pieces of Treasure act on the inner organs and are called Nei Kung, or internal movements.

As always breathing is important. Before you begin these movements, you should breathe deeply into the abdomen three times. With each breath, inhale fresh air through the nose and exhale stale air through the mouth.

TWO HANDS PUSH UP TO HEAVEN *(Figure 94)*

"Two Hands Push up to Heaven" is derived from the *I Ching* diagram *Ch'ien*, meaning Heaven. The exercise benefits the "triple heater." Triple heater is the terminology of Chinese medical science for three internal regions of the body. The "upper heater" extends from the entrance of the stomach up to the chest cavity and is associated with the respiratory system. The "middle heater" is related to the stomach and the intestines of the digestive system. And the "lower heater" describes the area from the stomach downward, which includes the reproductive and urinary systems. The purpose of Two Hands Push up to Heaven is to breathe in more oxygen and exhale more carbon dioxide. It also stimulates blood that is stagnating in the abdomen. Because the whole body stretches in this movement, Two Hands Push up to Heaven can also lengthen the ligaments.

94

1. Separate your legs so that your feet stand parallel to each other at shoulder width.

2. With your hands close to your forehead, intertwine the fingers of your hands with the palms facing away from you.

3. Breathe in fresh air as you push your hands and arms upward over your head. As you inhale, raise your heels so that you stand on your toes.

4. Now lower your arms in front of you, while your fingers remain intertwined. As the arms descend, exhale and let your heels touch the ground—all as one motion.

5. Repeat this eight times.

DRAW BOW TO SHOOT BIRDS (LEFT AND RIGHT)

This form is symbolized in *I Ching* by *Ken* or "the mountain"—suggesting that the stance of your legs should be as strong and firm as a mountain. The movement strengthens your legs and extends the ligaments of the arms. It also helps you to concentrate your mind. The exercise is not strenuous, for it uses mental power rather than physical strength.

1. Keeping the body erect, begin by standing with your feet close together. Take a wide step with your left foot— wider than shoulder width—and stand low, as if you were riding a horse.

2. Raise your arms as if you were holding a bow in your right hand and an arrow poised in the left. Your body remains low and erect, and the head moves only slightly to the right so that the eyes may fix on your right thumb.

3. Hold your left arm at chest level with the forearm

parallel to the ground. Inhaling, let the breath and the mind sink to the abdomen as you pull back the drawstring of the imaginary bow with your left hand. As your left arm pulls back, move your body weight to your left leg. Exhale.

To perform the exercise from the right, reverse these movements—aiming the bow and arrow to the left and placing your weight to the right leg. As you shift from left to right to left again, simultaneously inhale and move the mind and weight to the center of the body.

RAISING HANDS ALTERNATELY TO HARMONIZE SPLEEN AND STOMACH
(Figure 95)

This movement is related to the *I Ching* trigram *K'un*, meaning stomach. By combining the movement, the mind, and the breathing, the exercise benefits the "middle heater" by acting upon the stomach and thus assisting the digestive system.

1. Place your feet together. As you inhale, move your left foot left, to about shoulder width. Stand firmly with a peaceful mind.
2. Raise your left hand, palm up, over your head. Inhale and direct the breath with the mind to the abdomen.
3. Now lower the left hand and exhale slowly.
4. Raise the right hand over your head in a similar fashion, inhaling. Lower the right hand while exhaling.
5. Repeat this swimming motion from three to seven times. Each movement of first one hand then the other is considered one complete cycle.

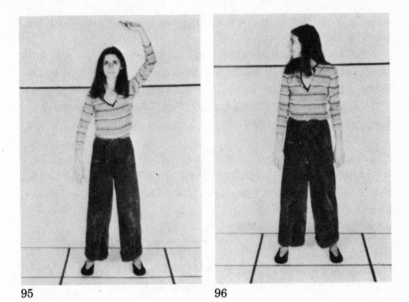

95   96

TURN HEAD LOOKING BACKWARD TO PREVENT RESPIRATORY DISEASE (LEFT AND RIGHT) *(Figure 96)*

This exercise is identified by the *I Ching* trigram *Tui*—alluding to the lungs. It is used to activate the nerves and the organs of the respiratory system. The neck and the spinal column contain three nerve lines: the central, peripheral, and autonomic nervous systems. This exercise strengthens these nerve lines and, in so doing, helps the inner organs.[3] Since the movement increases the activity of the nervous systems, such diseases as tuberculosis and bronchitis can be prevented.

1. Stand erect, with the feet shoulder width apart. Hold the head erect, eyes looking forward, and the tongue against the palate.

2. The shoulders should be relaxed. Let your arms hang

naturally at the sides, with the palms of the hands facing
toward the back.

3. Turn the head and the body all the way to the left and
backward in a single motion. Also look to the left and backward with the eyeballs.

4. Next, reverse this action: Direct the head and body to
the right and backward, as well as the eyeballs.

This exercise resembles Wave Hands Like Clouds, except that the hands remain at your sides and are not raised.
Beginners should only perform this movement three times,
to avoid damage to the body. In time, they can work their
way up to seven completed movements.

OPEN EYES WIDELY AND MAKE FISTS TO INCREASE ENERGY *(Figure 97)*

This form is represented by *Chen*, the *I Ching* trigram
for strength and anger. It uses deep breathing to restore
energy to the *tan t'ien* or lower abdomen. The *chi* then
travels through the spinal cord to the shoulders and arms.
As a result, energy is increased, blood circulation is accel-
erated, and the assimilation of body cells is improved.

1. Separate the feet a bit wider than shoulder width.
Lower your torso as if sitting astride a horse.

2. Raise your arms to shoulder height in front of you.
Extend them naturally, not stretched or tense. Clench your
fists and direct the mind and the *chi* to the *tan t'ien*.

3. Tighten the muscles of the anus. This directs the vitality and the *chi* up through the spine to the arms. Simultaneously open your eyes very wide and look forward. This
strengthens the eyeballs and thereby improves the vision.

4. Finally, return the vitality and the *chi* to the abdomen. When this has been accomplished, exhale very slowly.

97

Altogether, this is considered one completed cycle of Open Eyes Widely and Make Fists to Increase Energy. As with the previous exercise, the beginner should take care to perform the movement moderately, without much strain. At first, he should do the cycle only once. After much practice, he can gradually progress to three completed cycles without risk to his internal systems.

ROCKING FEET BACK AND FORTH TO PREVENT MANY DISEASES

The *I Ching* trigram *Sun*—representing this exercise—stands for the legs and arms. The movement brings resilience to the legs and to the spinal column. Thus it helps people who cannot bend easily or who suffer from rigid posture due to inflexibility. Many diseases can be prevented by this movement—including illnesses of the inner organs and such "external" problems as stiff joints or being unable to raise the arms overhead. By making the veins and arteries both softer and more pliant, the form also helps the circulation of the blood.

1. Stand erect but relaxed. The feet are placed together and the legs are resilient. As in T'ai Chi Ch'uan, the arms rest at the sides and the mind is at peace. Put the tongue against the palate. Direct the mind and the breathing to the *tan t'ien*.

2. Shift your weight to your toes, raising your heels from three to four inches off the floor.

3. In a continuous movement, shift your weight to your heels, raising the toes about two to three inches into the air.

4. Let the knees bend slightly as your feet rock forward and backward.

5. Do not perform this movement more than three to five times. To rock on the feet more often will cause strain.

ROTATE THE HEAD AND LOWER BACK TO CURE HEARTBURN

This movement is represented by *Li*—meaning heart and fire in the *I Ching*. It can make the whole body more relaxed and can increase the mobility of the limbs, the neck, and the lower back. The exercise can diminish heartburn, help the digestion, improve blood circulation, and make ligaments resilient.

1. Stand erect and move your left foot a little farther than shoulder width. Lower the trunk of the body as if you were riding a horse.

2. Rotate the lower back in a circle to the left. Repeat this motion three to five times in the same direction.

3. Simultaneously, rotate the head in a circle, also to the left. The movement should be fluid and relaxed.

4. Change the rotations of the head and lower back to the opposite direction. As before, repeat from three to five circles.

Five rotations to the left and five to the right constitute one complete cycle. As you become more adept at these exercises, you can work your way up to repeating the circles in either direction from seven to nine times.

TWO HANDS TOUCH FEET TO STRENGTHEN THE WAIST AND KIDNEYS *(Figure 98)*

K'an is the *I Ching* trigram for water, here referring to the kidneys. This form strengthens the legs and the spinal cord. It is of special benefit to the kidneys, for its stimulating movement prompts the excretion of wastes.

98

1. Stand erect with the feet a bit more narrow than shoulder width. Place the breath in the abdomen.

2. Bend the torso forward, stretching both arms in front of you, and try to touch your feet. Do not exert undue strain.

3. Very slowly, return to the erect posture.

4. Exhale slowly.

The movement should be slow and relaxed. Beginners should only perform it three times, later working up to five. If the blood pressure is not high, younger students can do the form seven times. However, aged people should only bend as far as they can with comfort and without unnecessary force or strain. People with high blood pressure, a history of heart attack, or like ailments should avoid this exercise altogether.

EXERCISES THAT CAN BE DONE IN BED

Many senior citizens who have stiff legs and bent backs can walk only with difficulty. This problem is caused by poor blood circulation. The ligaments are weak and stiff; therefore practicing movements to stretch the ligaments improves health and posture. Many gymnasiums and health clubs have machines to help stretch the ligaments, but it is easier to practice alone on a bed with a soft mattress.

The following exercises should be practiced every day, gently and without strenuous force, which can hurt the body. The performance can be stepped up slowly, so that you reach your goal in stages. I mentioned these exercises in *Taoist Health Exercise Book* (pp. 58–59). Now I will explain them in detail.

1. Stretch arms: slowly stretch your legs out in front; clasp your hands together, turning the palms upward; and stretch your arms gently as high as possible.

2. Stretch legs: slide your palms along the outside of your legs, and bend your body and head forward. When the legs and arms are fully extended, grasp the soles of the feet from the sides. Then return to a sitting position.

These exercises can be repeated ten to fifteen times. They should be practiced daily in the morning and evening. These exercises will stretch the ligaments and help reduce stiffness and hardening of the arteries and veins. They also strengthen the stomach and intestines, helping digestion and elimination; the kidneys, preventing kidney stones; and the testicles, preventing orchitis. They can help regulate urination, especially for older people, and increase the warmth of the body, particularly in winter.

Here is another exercise that should be done on a bed, where it is more comfortable to practice. Lie down on a bed with a pillow about two inches high. Separate your legs so they are the same distance apart as your shoulders.

1. Using the right hand, massage the area between your heart and stomach continuously, from left to right and to the left again, not too lightly and not too hard, about 80 to 100 times.

2. Massage the stomach, using the left hand to make a circle around the navel: left hand from left up, to the right (counterclockwise), down below the navel, and to the left, circle again. Continue slowly and gently 80 to 100 times.

3. Use the palm of the hand to cover the navel. Inhale through the nose, bringing the air down to the abdomen until it is full, and slowly exhale from the mouth. Inhale again until the abdomen is full. Use your mind to guide the *ch'i* along your legs to the soles of your feet. Then exhale gently from the mouth. Breathe again as before until the *ch'i* reaches the soles of the feet. Use your mind to guide

the *ch'i* slowly up along the inside of your legs through the perineum, reaching the abdomen again. If you have time you should practice several times a day or for longer periods. These exercises can improve the blood circulation. Let the *ch'i*, or breathing, go to every part of your body, making it warm and preventing disease.

SEATED BREATHING

PART 1

1. Sit down in a comfortable but firm chair whose seat is as high as your knees.

2. Place your hands on your knees and your feet squarely on the ground as far apart as your shoulders.

3. Breathe in through your nose as you lean forward, head down.

4. As you breathe in, raise the *ch'i* from the bottoms of your feet, through the inside of your legs, into the mortal cavity (below the genitals), then up through the body to the back, and then to the top of the head.

5. Raise your body and head back to the upright position, holding your breath, concentrating on the *ch'i* at the top of your head.

6. Exhale through your mouth; allow the vital energy to return to the mortal cavity.

Repeat this exercise nine times.

PART 2

1. Sitting, with your hands on your knees and feet flat on the floor, breathe in through the nose.

2. Lean forward, exhaling slowly through your mouth as you do.

3. Send the *ch'i* from the forehead through the front of the body through the abdomen, and then along the outside of the legs to the soles of the feet.

4. Sit up again and repeat this exercise nine times.

After the Seated Breathing exercise, stand up. Begin the Standing Exercise. It is best to have on loose garments (including undergarments) for this exercise.

STANDING EXERCISE

1. Standing, place your feet as wide apart as your shoulders, with both feet facing forward, parallel to each other. Concentrate your mind and your weight in the soles of your feet.

2. Your whole body should be erect and relaxed, with your arms hanging down naturally beside your legs, palms to the rear.

3. Your mind should be relaxed and quiet for two or three minutes.

4. Then begin to shake gently, both inside and outside. Your whole body should shake gently, both muscles and inner organs. Let your upper and lower teeth click together freely, and let your breathing be free.

Shake for two or three minutes.

Both the inner organs and the genitals shake freely. This can help prevent prostatitis, urinary tract inflammations and infections, and diseases of the testicles and vagina. You will feel very comfortable and relaxed. This same principle and movement is found in another exercise called Wai Tan Kung, meaning Exercise for Outside Elixir. In this exercise you stand with feet parallel, knees relaxed, arms hang-

ing loosely at sides. Shake the whole body, inside and outside—including tongue, fingers, genitals. This is a very
popular exercise in Taipei and in the Mainland, as well as in
America.

SITTING MEDITATION

Meditation relaxes the mind, rests the body, regulates
breathing and blood circulation, and, ultimately, improves
health. But there are so many different schools of meditation that the beginner may well become confused and dis-
heartened.

This is especially true of the elderly who mistakenly may
believe that they must adopt the lotus or half-lotus posture
in order to meditate. In the lotus position, a person sits
erect on a flat surface with the legs crossed, the feet resting
upon the thighs or calves. In the half-lotus, one foot is
placed in this position while the other remains between the
knee and the floor. The beginner or an older person has
great difficulty getting the feet in such a posture without
force, strain, and discomfort. Since it at first is a challenging position to sustain while meditating, such a person
might become very discouraged.

The method of meditation here proposed, however, is
much less demanding on the body and is easy to perform. It
requires that a person sit in a firm but comfortable chair,
with the feet flat on the floor and the open hands cupped
below the navel. The body should be relaxed but erect, the
mind in the quiet disposition of meditation.

First the mind (followed by the breathing, *chi*) sinks to
the abdomen to concentrate on the *tan t'ien*. Next, it moves
back to the kidney area or *Ming-Men* ("gate of life"). Now
the mind travels to the perineum, that sensitive region

between the anus and the genitals, which the Chinese know as *Hui-Yin*. Finally, the mind descends to the soles of the feet or *Yung-Ch'uan* (bubbling spring). Where the mind goes the breathing follows. Thus, the breathing should be slow and even, at a rate of about twenty units per minute. This form of meditation, though very easy to do, is very effective.

NOTES

1. Shi T'iao M'ei, *T'ai Chi Ch'uan: Internal and External Study* (in Chinese) (Taiwan: Hua Shin, 1959), pp. 15–19.
2. In the book cited immediately below, I also refer to the Pa Kua exercises. However, there I describe the exercises to be done in the sitting position. Here, we are studying the Pa Kua exercises as performed standing up, which makes them easier to do. Da Liu, *Taoist Health Exercise Book* (New York: Links Books, 1974), p. 47.
3. For more details on the relationship between the central nervous system and the inner organs, see Chapter 2.

CHAPTER 7:

HEALTH IN DAILY LIFE

Just as the plant needs soil, water, sunshine, and fertilizer in order to be healthy and grow strong, human beings have needs that are fundamental to their survival. External needs include food, clothing, shelter, and daily activity.

Care, however, should be taken to strike a suitable balance between tending too little and too much to these external needs. While the peoples of underdeveloped nations struggle to sustain themselves in these vital areas, those in industrial nations suffer from excessive overeating and the wasteful purchasing of unnecessary goods. There is an ancient Chinese saying, "People who want longevity should keep four empties." ("Empty" in this instance means being filled to only about 70 percent of capacity.) First, the mind should be free of thought. It should not dwell on the joys and sorrows of the past or the fantasies and fears of the future. Let the mind rest and be peaceful for mental health. Second, the stomach should not be stuffed with food. A poor diet abuses the stomach and causes disease. Third, the kitchen should be empty. Rather than store large quantities of food, buy only what will be used soon. This helps keep the kitchen clean and averts spoilage of food. Excess food attracts roaches and rats, thus promoting more harm and disease. Finally, keep the living quarters empty. Rooms cluttered with furniture and bric-a-brac stagnate the air and are difficult to keep clean.

The sections below describe the importance of food, clothing, shelter, and daily activity to health, and emphasize the need for suitably balanced maintenance of each.

FOOD

Confucius long ago said that the superior man does not eat too much. And in many civilized countries, doctors advise people to control food intake. Too strict a diet, however, can be harmful. Severe fasting brings discomfort and fails to provide the body with needed nutrition. A more selective choice of foods and a moderate diet are best for health.

It is good to regulate eating to certain times of the day. Li Ch'ing Yuen, who it is said lived for 250 years, recommended that people not overeat on summer nights and that they eat heartily on winter mornings. Because summer heat makes a person tired, overeating in the evening causes stagnation, whereas the added calories of a good breakfast help combat the cold of winter. Excessive drinking in the middle of the night is also discouraged.

Food should be fresh, rich in nutrients, and clean. Avoid overcooking foods, for this destroys vitamins that can benefit the body. If the temperature of the food is too cold, it will cause the body distress; if too hot it will harm the teeth and stomach. Be moderate in the size of food portions. Overeating taxes the stomach and the intestines. As a short-term consequence, indigestion and other ailments described in Chapter 2 may occur. Over a long period of time, overeating contributes to the gaining of weight, high blood pressure, and the possibility of heart attack.

Moderation and care are important after a meal. After eating, brush the teeth to rid the mouth of food particles that can cause tooth decay. Avoid strenuous exercise—both physical and mental—immediately after eating. A more gentle activity—such as going for a walk—is advisable. Office workers who haven't got the time to take a stroll after lunch can walk in the office or try a few movements of T'ai Chi Ch'uan to help digestion.

CLOTHING

The primary purpose of clothing is protection for good health. Because clothing protects the body from cold, rain, intense sun, and so on, it helps prevent illness. Therefore, clothing should be kept clean, dry, and suitable for changing weather conditions.

Unfortunately, many people underestimate or disregard the health function of clothing. Some dress merely to cover themselves while others are solely interested in adornment. They often fail to realize that "stylish" clothes can actually impair the health. Rough fabrics can chafe the skin. Very tight clothes hinder the blood circulation. Even extremely loose clothing can impede walking and work and is difficult to keep clean in rainy weather.

There are appropriate forms of dress that can protect the various parts of the body.

The head is important, because it contains the brain and most of the sense organs. A hat protects the head from wind, rain, snow, cold, and bright sun. It can help prevent ear infection and headache. The hat should be a suitable size and appropriate for prevailing weather conditions.

A scarf can protect the neck and the upper chest without inhibiting the breathing. This protection benefits the throat and lungs. Western man protects his chest from drafts with a vest. In China, women wear a piece of cloth across the chest to protect the bust and midriff. Fashion sometimes dictates that women expose the midriff. This is very bad, since exposing the navel to winds leaves the body more vulnerable to illness in the stomach, intestines, and lungs.

The waist and lower back are very sensitive, since they contain the center of the nerve line and many intricate bones. Chilly winds can cause painful backache if this area is left unprotected. For women, the lower back is especially sensitive. Exposure to cold may induce irregular or painful menstrual periods. Long skirts or trousers are good protection for women.

The healthful advantages of shoes cannot be taken lightly. The feet are as important to the body as the foundation is to a building. The feet affect all other activity, and injury to them should be avoided. Therefore, it is good sense to pick shoes not for style but for protection of the foot. Shoe size should be accurate. If shoes fit poorly, the feet will suffer. Inflexible material can also harm the feet. Avoid high heels, so that walking will be more balanced and natural. Shoe shines are attractive but not very useful; just be sure that the shoes are clean and dry to ensure healthy feet.

The umbrella is portable protection from bad weather. As the Western saying goes, "The wise man carries his umbrella even on a sunny day." This means that he is prepared if the weather changes unexpectedly. The umbrella can also be used as a walking stick to improve balance. When sitting, place the tip of the umbrella between the feet and rest both hands on its handle. This will help improve the posture of the back.

SHELTER

Our dwelling places are like strongholds: We look to them for both physical and mental security, as well as for rest and socializing. The rooms should be clean, quiet, dry, and protected from extremes of weather so that we can avoid diseases.

In modern times, conveniences like air conditioning and central heating promise increased comfort but can promote disease instead, due to human carelessness and neglect. Although people enjoy the comforts of air conditioning during the day and early evening, they can catch cold if they leave the air conditioner on too high before going to bed. When the body is asleep, it has less strength to combat cold; meanwhile, chilly air continually lowers the room temperature. Since night air is usually cooler than that of the daytime, the air conditioner should be turned down at night or turned off completely.

In contrast, a heated home is comfortable in the wintertime. If the rooms are too warm in the evening, however, members of a family—especially children—may neglect to cover themselves adequately when they go to bed. In community buildings, the heat is turned off or lowered after midnight. The chill of dawn leaves the unblanketed sleeper susceptible to colds, flu, or pneumonia. Thus it is wise to lower the temperature an hour or so before retiring and to dress warmly for bed. If living in a community building where the rooms are too hot, briefly open the windows to adjust the temperature. With more care, moderate and healthy temperatures can be achieved.

Comfort and health require a clean and quiet environment. House plants provide not only decoration but a benefit to health. Both plants and cross-ventilation freshen the air with added oxygen. Rooms should be clean and sparsely furnished. If possible, keep cats, dogs, birds, and similar domestic pets out of the living quarters. They spoil the air, disturb a restful atmosphere with their noise, and shed fur or feathers on furniture and food.

Safety is another concern. Keep vulnerable doors and windows locked for protection.

When the environment is too hot, the body soon feels discomfort. The appetite is dampened, as is the perspiring skin. Although the body feels more exhausted, sleeping is difficult. This physical fatigue brought on by intensive heat weakens the body's defenses against disease.

Modern technology has provided the means to escape such heat or at least make the situation more bearable. Fans and air conditioners lower the temperature in a room. But take care not to make the room too cold too fast, especially if you have been in the heat for a long time. Nor should an electric fan's path of air blow directly on the body, for it can stiffen the muscles and make you catch cold. The evening is usually cooler and provides air that is at least as fresh as that filtered through an air conditioner.

A too cold environment also impairs the health. Chilled air can induce harsh coughs, nasal congestion, fever, runny eyes, body aches, phlegm in the lungs, plain physical discomfort, and more severe forms of the common cold such as influenza and pneumonia.

Again, modern heating systems make it easier than in the past to control room temperature and thereby avoid chills. Another good measure is to wear warmer clothing. But be careful not to perspire too much under sweaters or thermal underwear, lest the conditions be present for a cold or even frostbite.

Children and the elderly are especially susceptible to coughs and colds caused by strong winds, because their physical resistance is not too strong. Respiratory diseases can result from exposure to winds, as can aching muscles and menstrual cramps. The best protection is to stop up all drafts within a house and to cover the nose and mouth when outside. Do not breathe directly against the wind, since this increases the risk of harm to internal organs. The wind also carries particles of dirt, insects, pollution, and small objects, which may blow into the eye at high speed. To shield the eyes, wear wind goggles or sun glasses.

Humidity occurs when the air is heavy with moisture. Muggy weather brings about sneezing, itchy eyes, and labored breathing. In China, we used to heat damp air with coal fires. Nowadays, machines called "dehumidifiers" can pull the wetness out of the air by turning it into water.

Air that is too dry is unhealthy, too. It affects the eyes and throat unpleasantly, parches the skin and the interiors of the nostrils, and cracks or chaps the lips. Predictably, technology has invented the "humidifier" to add moisture to an arid room in the form of steam.

Being outside in too much water—in rain, snow, and so on—is harmful. Indoors, the threat of dampness is present in dank, poorly ventilated rooms or basements. And remember the previous warning about the unhealthy conditions caused by excessive perspiration, especially when combined with extreme cold or wind. Extreme wetness results in skin irritation, coughs and colds, rheumatism, and even tuberculosis. If you get stuck in a storm, towel yourself dry and change your clothes immediately.

As we have seen, technology has offered us many ways to shield ourselves from the extremes of weather. But people still suffer from illnesses brought on by these external forces and thus cannot easily relax the mind. Most often, such illnesses are due to human carelessness and neglect. For example, I went out into a heavy downpour to visit a teacher friend. When he saw that I had gotten drenched by the rain, he advised me to change out of my wet clothes immediately. I refused, assuring him that I would be all right. Within a month, I had rheumatism.

DAILY ACTIVITY

Daily physical activity has been the subject of many of my books—including my *Taoist Health Exercise Book*[1] and the forthcoming "T'ai Chi Ch'uan and Meditation." In this text, we shall examine those aspects of daily activity that relate more specifically to older people.

Walking, standing, sitting, and reclining are matters of common practice for everyone. However, proper and healthful approaches to these daily activities are often neglected. Taoist and Confucian sages have long recommended simple ways to improve one's health and lengthen one's life. A maxim about how everyday posture contributes to these ends goes as follows:

> Walk like the wind.
> Stand like the pine.
> Sit like the bell.
> Sleep like the bow.

Too much strain when walking consumes unnecessary energy and unduly tires the walker. A light and natural gait—flowing as the wind—is more relaxing. The pine tree stands erect, firm, steady—not bent or inclined to any side. If possible, stand with the body's weight on one leg and the other foot "light" or weightless. When this arrangement grows tiring, shift the weight to the other foot. Such a practice aids circulation and removes tension from the shoulders and neck. The temple bells of China are long and straight, not curved like those in the West. Thus, even when sitting, the spine should be erect. Rigidity should be avoided when sleeping, however. The bow is curved, suggesting that the reclining body should bend in a relaxed—rather than corpselike—position. Sleeping in this manner facilitates breathing and keeps joints loose.

We have already mentioned Li Ch'ing Yuen in this chapter. This sage, who lived 250 years, likened some of the same postures to commonly known animals:

> Walk like the crane.
> Sit like the tortoise.
> Sleep like the dog.

Many people walk very badly. With tense, stooped shoulders and head down, they seem to point themselves forward as their feet shuffle along the ground. In contrast, the crane's head is erect and looking forward, not in a stoop. When walking, it puts one foot flat on the ground while the other is weightless in the air. This posture is similar to that used in T'ai Chi Ch'uan. The body is balanced, with the weight in the legs rather than in the neck and shoulders. Stooping while walking puts pressure on the heart, increases the probability of losing one's balance, and is generally uncomfortable. By placing the weight of the body on the foot that touches the ground, the tension caused by stooping is alleviated. As in T'ai Chi Ch'uan, one foot is heavy while the other is weightless in the air. Because the whole foot touches flat when walking, its veins and arteries are pressed and relaxed to improve blood circulation. Such are the advantages of emulating the walk of the crane.

The tortoise, too, can teach us by its example. This animal is remarkably quiet and passive. It shuns all stimuli and shrinks from aggressors. When sitting, the human should also be quiet and relaxed, but maintaining a straight spine. Do not be distracted by noise or physical surroundings.

In contrast, the dog is alert even when sleeping and can awaken easily when disturbed. Sound sleepers often fail to protect themselves from changes in the temperature or weather. Light sleeping is also good protection from thieves, fires, and like emergencies.

But the simile of Li Ch'ing Yuen refers more to body position than just alertness. The dog sleeps with its neck straight, its forelegs out, and the hindquarters bent. People who sleep with the neck bent or strained suffer painfully when they wake up, while sleeping with the hands over the heart is said to cause nightmares. Copying the position of a sleeping dog, however, forestalls both physical and mental discomfort. The body is naturally relaxed so that the blood circulation is free and not hindered by tense muscles and rigidity. Inner organs of the body, too, are more apt to function better when the sleeper adopts this posture.

These, then, are general views on the proper use of daily activity to benefit health and longevity. With this brief introduction to theories about walking, standing, sitting, and reclining, let us now examine the practical application of each. Our study will include an additional activity—squatting—which is of special help to people suffering from backache.

WALKING

When traveling today, a person has numerous modes of transportation from which to choose, but one should not underestimate the importance of simply walking.

People walk short distances for everyday tasks, even if it is just to go from a living room chair to the front seat of a car. But walking can be used to increase physical fitness—aiding digestion and blood circulation—and mental relaxation. Walking as exercise is favored among Taoists and Buddhists. Taoists perform walking meditation, whereas Buddhists liken walking to the motion of a floating cloud. Both sects apply this activity in conjunction with sitting meditation to achieve the goals of health and longevity. Thus we see the functions of walking from the commonest level to the most advanced.

With such a variety of purposes, each kind of walking involves special considerations. When simply walking on the street, the pedestrian should keep the mind relaxed and clear, while taking care to avoid accidents. Pollution is a challenge to city dwellers when they walk. Rather than cross city streets at the intersectons or the middle of the block, they should cross slightly above the intersection in order to escape the densest concentration of engine fumes but still be able to check traffic conditions. Practicing light breathing at these times minimizes the effect of pollutants on the body. Sunlight is another factor for everyday walking. In the winter, try to walk in the sunshine as much as possible. But during the summer, refrain from exposing the skin to heavy doses of intense sun.

Taking a stroll is different in intent and practice from walking on the street. Its purpose is mental and physical relaxation, in the morning, for example, after a meal or before retiring for the evening. This is a quiet form of exercise and should involve no strain or unnecessary excitement. Parks or the countryside provide the best surroundings, because they contain trees and vegetation and are uncrowded. When strolling, walk slowly and leave serious thoughts behind. Because there is no set destination for this type of walking, the stroller is free to turn in any direction, pause at will, and generally follow the whims of the moment. While this freedom aids mental relaxation, be sure to let the muscles and joints relax as well while walking. If practiced regularly—with a mind to traveling about the same distance for the same amount of time daily— strolling proves to be a simple and healthy form of exercise that can be of particular benefit to the elderly or the ailing.

Strenuous exercise is not recommended for the ill or for older people, since it may result in injury or strain. However, jogging, a controlled form of slow running, strikes a middle ground between strolling and exercises that are physically demanding. Although jogging has enjoyed increased popularity in the West over the past few years, ancient Taoist writings long ago made mention of *shieng chio* or meditative jogging. Taoist jogging and T'ai Chi Ch'uan share common principles: the peaceful mind, the relaxed, erect upper body, and transfer of weight from one leg to the other. Jogging can be performed slowly at the beginning, and its pace can eventually be increased.[2] Clearly, such a disciplined form of walking differs dramatically from that of the average pedestrian.

STANDING

Although it is used less frequently than walking and sitting, standing is a daily activity that remains a major factor in good health and long life.

Taoists practice meditative standing. Fixing the eyes forward without intense glaring, the mind and the breathing are put deep into the abdomen. The tongue is placed against the palate to stimulate the production of saliva. The upper body should be erect but with the shoulders relaxed and both arms hanging naturally at the sides. Unlocking the knee joints, the bent legs assume the brunt of the body's weight. Eighty to ninety percent of this pressure is concentrated in one leg while the other remains light or weightless. When the leg needs rest, the weight is shifted to the other leg. In Taoist terminology, this alternation is between *yin* (heavy) and *yang* (light).

It is better to perform meditative standing in a park, a garden, or the countryside. Dense foliage provides fresh oxygen and the blossoms of flowers invigorate. Inhale and swallow this vitalizing atmosphere deep into the abdomen. The months of spring and autumn have the most moderate temperature and the clearest air.

Admittedly, meditative standing is a very specialized

form of standing, but you can apply aspects of meditative standing to everyday situations. When standing during a conversation or waiting in a line, do not lean or slouch. Good posture, a peaceful mind, and (when possible) pleasant surroundings should be recognized as fundamentals of healthy standing.

SITTING

Sitting is a common daily activity, but too much sitting makes the body stiff. At regular intervals—every hour or half hour—the sitting person should walk about, stand, or perform simple exercises. This will relax the muscles, loosen the joints, and assist blood circulation. Alternating between sitting and moving about on a regular basis is especially prudent for the elderly and those who are convalescing from illness.

The office worker and the musician are members of two professions that share a common problem: They are seldom permitted to indulge in regulated intervals of sitting and exercise. Nonetheless, they should assume a healthy posture and attempt more restricted forms of body motion. With the tongue against the roof of the mouth, sit with the head and spine erect but without rigidity or tension. Typists who cannot leave their desks for long periods of time are especially susceptible to backaches and headaches. They should move the shoulders in a rotating fashion to limber up tense muscles and loosen up by occasionally turning at the waist to alleviate additional muscle strain. They can also shift weight from one haunch to the other and change sitting position when the circulation seems inhibited.

Whether sitting for work or rest, the height of the chair is a factor. It should be neither higher nor lower than knee level.[3]

RECLINING AND SLEEPING

Reclining and sleeping are essential to all—the aged and the infirm in particular—as a means to conserve energy. Many Taoists have turned to meditative sleeping to augment health and longevity.

If people experience difficulty getting enough rest or sleeping easily, the problem may be a faulty mattress. Young persons need a hard mattress for firm support and to promote good posture. However, the bones of older people are more sensitive and dry. While slats of wood under the mattress will provide support, therefore, their mattress should be soft and comfortable to prevent undue pain in the bones. Such mattresses are of particular value to persons who have to be confined to bed for long periods of time.

If insomnia persists, get up and walk a while. Alternate between sitting and standing. To relax the mind and the body, breathe deeply into the abdomen. Soon it should be less difficult to sleep.

My *Taoist Health Exercise Book* contains more information about meditative sleeping[4] and preferred sleeping positions.[5]

SQUATTING

In Chapter 2, it was pointed out that the spine is naturally straight during the childhood years but that it can become badly stooped as a person grows older, causing severe backaches. A good method for alleviating this pain and correcting bad posture is squatting.

Squatting can be a healthful daily activity to promote longevity. Younger people can squat daily to improve straightness of the spine, but older people—most notably those suffering from extreme stooping or back ailments—

should perform squatting with caution and care to protect themselves against further complications.

The methods for regular and meditative squatting are detailed in my *Taoist Health Exercise Book*.[6]

A final point should be made about daily activities as they affect health and longevity. It has been illustrated in this chapter how moderate exercise involving even the most common daily activities can benefit both the mind and the body. But it must be emphasized that abuse of the faculties through overexertion or lack of temperance can cause stress, tax the energy, and do physical harm. Older readers should take special note of the advice below, since they may overdo willfully or unintentionally and thereby hurt themselves.

True, we all take part in such common daily activities as walking, standing, sitting, and sleeping or reclining. But too much running or walking can injure the ligaments, while excessive standing hurts the bones. The circulatory system—most particularly, the pulse and blood flow—can be hampered by unrelieved sitting. And oversleeping tends to make the head groggy and curtails lucid thinking.

Temperance is recommended in other daily activities as well. Do not overuse your eyes by watching too much television or reading for too long without a rest. This intense and unrelieved staring hampers vitality. Control your tongue also, for nonstop talkers damage vitality, too, and impede the healthful production of saliva. Nor should you overeat, for this will affect the inner organs and threaten good health and well-being.

In short, be moderate in all you do. Do not abuse your body by too much or too little activity. With care and common sense, you can extend health for long life.

NOTES

1. (New York: Links Books, 1974).
2. For further details, see *ibid.*, pp. 68–72.
3. For more details, consult *ibid.*, pp. 39–41.
4. *Ibid.*, pp. 22–24.
5. *Ibid.*, pp. 24–27.
6. *Ibid.*, pp. 63–64.

CHAPTER 8:

SELF-TREATMENT: THE METHODS OF MASSAGE AND ACUPRESSURE

The Chinese characters *an* (apply pressure) and *mo* (rub wounds or painful areas of the body) combine as *An Mo* to signify the Western concept of massage. A massage is a series of manual presses and manipulations applied to tissues and muscles of the human body. It can also relieve physical suffering and disabilities, as it prolongs health by toning up the nervous system, glands, organs, and joints.

Chinese massage is related to the ancient medical sciences of acupuncture and acupressure. They share the belief that there are points in the body that correspond to energy complexes of the internal organs. By massaging these points, the *chi* and blood circulation can flow more easily to the desired location—for example, the heart, liver, bladder, kidney, gall bladder, large and small intestines, lungs, neural centers of energy and warmth. Every nation is known to have its own massaging technique, but only Chinese massage takes these meridians into account.

In the beginning, Chinese massage was so simple to do that it could easily be self-administered. Later, as skill in its practice matured, specialists developed new methods and physicians began to massage people rather than have them do so for themselves. Better than 4,000 years ago, the Yellow Emperor (Hwang Ti) and his officer Ch'i Po were known to possess ten medical volumes related to An Mo. By the time of the T'ang Dynasty (618–905 A.D.), the government established the health posts of An Mo doctor and An Mo instructor, so that students could be trained in new and old massaging techniques. During the Ming Dynasty (1368–1628 A.D.), the *Book of An Mo* cited eight methods of massage—including, among others, pressing alone, rubbing alone, pressing and rubbing combined, pinching, shaking, and slapping or pounding.

The history of Chinese massage—both that performed on oneself and that administered to another—spans many centuries. I personally believe that either method of massaging is acceptable and effective. In this chapter, we shall limit ourselves to techniques that can be self-administered.

Self-administered massage is not only for the ill or infirm. It can be done in conjunction with many common activities during the day. When you rise in the morning, awaken the body and spirit with a general massage. After a meal, massage the stomach, heart, and chest to help digestion. Massaging the body after physical exercise restores the balance of yin and yang. If you are tired after work, a massage can help alleviate physical and mental stress. Localize the massage to those areas of the body that are most affected by your occupation. For example, people who walk most of the day should rub their legs; sedentary workers should massage their backs. A hot bath aids blood circulation. Massaging after a bath augments this improved blood circulation as it helps to dry the skin. Bedtime is the last opportunity of the day to take advantage of this practice. Massage the whole body to relieve tension in the body and the mind and to get to sleep more easily. If this is done at least once a day, you can make your body much healthier, stimulate blood circulation, improve nutrition by aiding the digestion, and make the skin tissue smoother.

Before you massage, make sure your body is clean and

dry, so as not to rub dirt and moisture into the pores of the skin. This is especially true of the sense organs located in the head. The best cleansing agent for the eyes and nose is borax solution. If this is unavailable, warm salt water will do. Begin by cleaning both the inside and the outside of the nose. An eye cup or a daub of cotton can be used to cleanse the eyes with cool salt water or borax solution. This practice prevents or deters itching. Brush the teeth and rinse out the mouth to rid it of food particles. Do not just wash behind the ears; use a piece of paper or toweling to dry the inside of the ear as well. If something obstructs one of these organs it can do great damage, affecting one's daily activities.

According to the medical books of China, illness should be treated before it leads to more serious complications. The longer a person waits to have a health problem tended to, the more difficult it is to achieve a cure. The wisdom of preventive medicine can be inferred from the writings of Lao Tzu (Chapter 64):

> When chaos has not yet appeared, it is easy to maintain peace. When portents have not yet appeared, it is easy to devise measures. When a thing is brittle, it can be easily broken. When a thing is minute, it can be easily dispersed.[1]

Self-treatment is one form of preventive medicine. More technical than massage, self-treatment is nonetheless more effective for people who detect early symptoms of illness. Of course, if the symptoms remain or worsen, consult a physician. Once the doctor has diagnosed the actual ailment, a regimen of doctor's care and self-treatment can ensue.

In China, the refinements of Western medicine are not available to all, especially those who live in far-off rural villages. While there exist many skilled physicians in

China, these country people often rely on persons of more general medical knowledge. Like the Druids of Europe before the coming of Christianity, these healers—called "barefoot doctors"—depend on the herbs and folkways of the past. They pack their herbs and acupuncture equipment in boxes, place the boxes at either end of a pole, and balance their belongings on their shoulder as they walk from village to village. In a recent New York *Times Book Review*, the book *A Barefoot Doctor's Manual*,[2] was received with curiosity and some condescension by the Western physician Michael Halberstam.[3] While it must be conceded that the barefoot doctors' methods are simpler and less sophisticated than those used in the West, it should also be recognized that treatment by a barefoot doctor is frequently effective.

During the last few years, Westerners have learned about the ancient Chinese practice of acupuncture. This medical system treats disease by sticking needles into the points on the meridians. Less known is a similar medical science called acupressure. Its Chinese characters are *chih* (finger) and *ya* (pressure). Thus, Chih Ya involves pressing the meridian points with the fingers rather than sticking pins into them. But acupressure should not be equated with simple massage. Massage is applied directly to ailing parts of the body, while the practitioner of acupressure can, for example, treat indigestion by touching a point on the patient's hand or foot instead of the abdomen.

A basic form of acupressure can be self-administered. However, professional acupressure doctors possess more intricate healing power. *Chi* stored in the *tan t'ien* becomes a concentrated form of immense energy. The acupressure physician directs this force to his fingers. When he touches the patient, the energy is transferred. As it penetrates the patient's body, it stimulates blood circulation and unclogs stagnation, much as a strong current undams a river.

The best acupressure experts practice with the *chi* or inner energy every day for several years in order to accumulate ever more power in their hands, rather as an electric generator stores and produces power. This observation implies that there are specialists of various degrees of expertise and effectiveness. Different practitioners use their own techniques. So even though the same meridians may receive acupressure to treat the same ailment, two acupressure doctors can get different results by working on the same point or the same result from working on two different points.

Nonetheless, the results of such treatments can be startling. A friend of mine, Dr. Chia Lin Song, has a very powerful hand. He studied boxing many years at the Shao Lin temple. His acupressure treatments have cured ailments or alleviated conditions that Western physicians have considered incurable. For example, one of my students suffered terribly badly from a menstrual problem. Not even her father, a respected physician for twenty years, could help her. When she went to a hospital for relief, she was advised to undergo a hysterectomy. Instead, she went to Dr. Song and received immediate relief. She continues to get acupressure care each month at the time of her period.

The history of acupressure contains countless such anecdotes, going back thousands of years. During the reign of Hwang Ti, his troops were engaged in a bitter war with barbarians called Ch'ih Yu. There were many wounded in battle, and they suffered from bad weather and lack of supplies. Acupressure was used, however, to treat the ill and the infirm on the battlefield. By the time of the Warring States (403 B.C.–221B.C.), civil war was so rampant that many new forms of Chih Ya evolved to ease the pain of those who fought. Some of these were a great improvement and became popular among civilians in times of peace.

It is said that during the Period of the Warring States, one Kung Sun Chin was wounded in the back, which began to swell badly. By running madly, he escaped capture. One of his friends saw him and, not knowing he was wounded, jokingly punched his back. Kung Sun Chin looked around at his friend and immediately his back felt much better. By the next day the wound had disappeared.

Kung Sun Chin decided to study the reason for his cure. By experimenting on himself, he discovered many meridians and cavities in the body. Through years of experimenting, he found the use of acupressure to be little different from that of acupuncture. He created his own system working for both soldiers and civilians and made his living from the practice and teaching of this technique. Later on, he used his fingers, which concentrated the energy better than the fist. Over many years he improved his inner strength and used this intrinsic energy, which had been acquired through his knowledge of fighting, to penetrate points on the patient's body. He learned to propel the blood circulation, warming the cold points and curing diseases. This was more effective than the use of needles or muscular strength.

He researched the occurrence of many illnesses that arose due to hindrances in the blood circulation. He used the nerve line to find the source of the pain. He discovered that several nerve lines meet together at crossroads; at these points stimulation was applied and effective results were produced.

However, this method of healing eventually became a means of killing as well. A form of acupressure called Tien Mo (point of the pulse) was devised, by which an assailant would store up more powerful energy than necessary. He could then touch the pulse or meridian points of an enemy and maim or even kill him. Different touch points brought different results. One method killed immediately; another delayed death for a few days. Still another could merely paralyze the victim's body or strike him mute. The obvious martial advantage of Tien Mo was that—since the murder weapon was merely a touch of the hand—no clues remained by which the cause of death could be determined.

When the Han people revolted against the Manchurian Dynasty (1644–1910 A.D.), Tien Mo became such a common and lethal practice that the government forbade its being studied. However, the art of Tien Mo has been kept alive in secret among the peasantfolk of China.

Perhaps the strongest evidence that Tien Mo is still practiced can be found in the case of Bruce Lee. As a strong and skillful Chinese boxer, Bruce Lee defeated many Eastern and Western opponents. He became known in the West as a cult hero due to his masterful displays of Kung Fu and similar martial arts from China. At the height of his popularity, he experienced a brief period of discomfort and mysteriously died at the age of thirty-two. Medical examination found no indication of wounds or disease. Many suspect he was a victim of Tien Mo.

Tien Mo is not the only lethal variety of acupressure. If a person is frightened enough, a light pat of the hand or thrust of the fist can harm him. Some believe that the experienced assassin can hurt his victim by mere thought—without even touching him—but this borders on mere legend.

MASSAGE

Here are some practical techniques of self-administered massage that help stimulate and relax the extremities and joints, thereby benefiting the inner organs.

HAND MASSAGE

The hands contain intricate networks of arteries, veins, and nerves. Many of the meridians relating to the inner organs also cross the surfaces of the hands and fingers. Thus, massage that relaxes the hands has a direct effect on the blood circulation and nervous system and also affects the inner organs indirectly through the meridians.

Various kinds of hand massage can be easily performed whenever you wash and dry your hands. Rub the palms together. Then hold the right hand around the left. Turn and twist the left hand as you move the hands vigorously. Then change hands and repeat. Next, rub the hands together while intertwining the fingers. Finally, hold the left thumb with two fingers of the right hand and press all over the thumb, starting at the base and moving up to the tip. Repeat the same to massage each finger on both hands, one at a time.

FOOT MASSAGE

Like the hands, the feet contain many arteries, veins, and nerves. There are six meridians that run from the legs down to the feet: three yang meridians (affecting the stomach, bladder, and gall bladder) and three yin meridians (affecting the spleen, kidneys, and liver). The feet are even more important because they bear the whole weight of the body. Thus healthy feet are essential to good health generally; when there is a leg or foot trouble it has an effect on the whole body, on the blood circulation, digestion, even the heart and brain.

With this in mind, be careful to keep your feet in good condition. Wear shoes of the proper size, and when the weather is cold, try to wear shoes that will keep your feet warm. The methods of foot massage are best practiced upon wakening and before leaving bed in the morning. Rub the feet together, sole against instep. Then use the middle of the ball of the foot (referred to in Chinese writings as the "bubbling spring" to rub against the other foot. Then use the arch to massage the side of the foot and ankle. First do the left foot, then repeat the procedure on the right. This very simple relaxing practice can be a great help in releasing the body from sleep and in clearing the mind. It is relaxing, yet stimulating.

If you have time, you should also massage the toes. These deserve special attention since they perform work whenever we walk or stand but are often confined in shoes and don't get much exercise. They can become stiff and unable to bend, causing pain and tension when we walk. To stimulate the toes, use the right thumb and index finger to press all along the left big toe from bottom to top. Repeat with each left toe and then change hands and feet. Then rub the big toe and the second toe together vigorously. The three small toes will follow after the second toe.

Foot massage can be repeated several times a day if desired. Through regular massage and exercise, the feet become flexible and walking becomes easier.

WRIST MASSAGE

Apply the tip of the right thumb to the top side of the left wrist and rub firmly. Then rub the entire wrist area gently with the whole hand. Repeat the same procedure on the right wrist. By relaxing the wrist and stimulating blood circulation, one can cure arthritis, rheumatism, and other diseases that make the wrist and arm sore and stiff.

ELBOW MASSAGE

Place the thumb on the inner part of the elbow, the four fingers on the bone, and rub gently four or five times. Then rub the area with the whole hand.

KNEE MASSAGE

Just after rising in the morning, rub the knee region with a warm hand. This will make the whole leg and foot warm, stimulate blood circulation, prevent stiffness, and cure arthritis and rheumatism.

ACUPRESSURE

Here are some practical techniques of self-administered acupressure that can effectively cure minor ailments and relieve pain.

FOR HEADACHE

Apply pressure behind the knees of both legs in such a way as to form a triangle, with your head at the apex. The thumbs should be placed on the shin bones, and the four fingers behind the knees. The main pressure should be exerted through the middle fingers.

Another way of curing a headache, particularly when pain is in the front of the head, is to grasp each wrist with the four fingers of the opposite hand and apply pressure.

FOR STOMACH ACHE

Interlock the fingers of both hands and press down with both thumbs on a point three inches above the navel. Apply this pressure continuously for five to ten minutes.

Another method involves pressing with two fingers on a point below each knee. The points must be accurately located, however.

FOR LIVER TROUBLE

Push in on the left side under the ribs with three fingers. At the same time press the right palm flat against the rib cage. Continue the pressure for five to ten minutes.

FOR COUGHING, TOOTHACHE, AND HEADACHE

Press down with the right index finger on the fleshy part of the left hand between the thumb and index finger. At the same time, use the left thumb to press down on the same part of the right hand. Use strong pressure and continue for five to ten minutes.

FOR FACIAL PAIN

Place the right thumb on the fleshy part of the underside of the left hand, and place the left thumb on the top of the right hand. Press with the right index finger on the point on the outer part of the wrist between the hand and the arm.

FOR SORE THROAT

Press inward at a 45-degree angle with all four fingers of both hands on both clavicles. Maintain medium pressure.

MOXA AND FIRE TREATMENT

In China, the practice of acupuncture and acupressure is often accompanied by the use of moxa, called *chiu* in Chinese. The methods generally involve applying heat to the acupuncture point after the needles have been removed. The purpose of this is to disperse any coldness and stagnation of the blood, diminish swelling, and restore to normal balance the blood circulation in the area. The heat is applied in various ways. One way is to put small pieces of ginger on the area to be treated, then heat by burning some dried leaves of the mugwort (moxa) plant, and placing them in contact with the skin. This can be done either by putting a small quantity of leaves in a metal container and placing it on the skin while the leaves are burning, or by heaping a tiny amount directly on the skin and carefully lighting it.

Although these methods are mainly used in connection with acupuncture, they can also be effective when practiced separately. It is not necessary to apply the heat to acupuncture points. It can also be applied directly to a painful point or area of the body: I have found, for example, that it is particularly good for alleviating the pains of arthritis and rheumatism.

Other methods of applying heat that do not involve the use of the moxa plant include "cupping," in which a fire is made in a small jar, and after the burning material is discarded, the jar is quickly cupped over the area to be heated. The idea is not only to apply heat but also that the thin dry hot air inside the cup will act to draw the poisons out of the affected area. The fire can be made by burning bits of paper inside the jar, or by carefully lighting a wick that has been soaked in alcohol and placed in the jar. The technique of cupping is of relatively recent origin. The ancient method is to place bamboo stalks in boiling water, and then after drying them off carefully, to press the ends against the skin. The hot thin air within the porous stalks have the same effect as the air in the jar.

NOTES

1. For a different translation, see James Legge, *The Texts of Taoism* (New York: Dover Publications, 1962), vol. I, p. 107.

2. *A Barefoot Doctor's Manual: The Translation of the Official Chinese Paramedical Manual* (Philadelphia: Running Press, 1977).

3. "Also Swat the Grasshopper," New York *Times Book Review*, May 22, 1977, p. 10.

CHAPTER 9

THE PREVENTION AND TREATMENT OF THE MAJOR DISEASES THROUGH EXERCISE AND MEDITATION

TAOIST TREATMENTS FOR CANCER

To understand the Taoist treatments for cancer it is helpful to see how Chinese people view the disease itself: specifically, how they represent it in their written language. Chinese words are called pictographs. A change in part of a pictograph alters its meaning, just as adding a prefix like *re-* or *in-* to a word in English alters its meaning. For example, if part of the pictograph for sickness is added to another pictograph, it can indicate the kind of sickness under discussion. I have studied several Chinese words for diseases related to cancer and have found their origins instructive. For instance, the pictograph for tumor, 瘤 , pronounced *liu*, consists of part of the pictograph for sickness added to the pictograph 留 , which means to detain

or keep. Thus *liu* means a sickness in which the blood is not
circulating but is stagnating or being kept in one area. It is
not poisonous or painful, but it gradually increases in size.

A second pictograph, 癰 , pronounced *yung* (meaning
"ulcer") is sometimes used for cancer. The Chinese diction-
ary gives a detailed explanation for this kind of sickness.
First the area becomes red and the swelling becomes bigger, after which it breaks and covers a larger area. If we
take part of the pictograph for sickness away and add earth
below, 壅 , it has the same pronunciation but now means
that the water does not flow freely; it is stagnating.

A third pictograph, 疽 , also used to signify ulcer, is
pronounced *chu*. When the ulcer is beginning it is not red,
swollen, or painful, but when it is broken it is more serious
and is similar to cancer. Many people have died from this
illness in China. If we remove a part of this pictograph,
adding water on the left side, 沮 , it means to stop.

All three of these pictographs are related to cancer, and
all three share as the crux of their definitions the stopping
or stagnation of the blood circulation. It becomes apparent
that the Chinese believe avoidance of this stagnation helps
prevent cancer, and this leads us directly to a consideration
of exercise as a cancer preventive.

The Japanese expert, Michio Kushi, recommended different exercises to treat different kinds of cancer, but in
my opinion T'ai Chi Ch'uan can prevent and treat any kind
of cancer. Through its gentle internal and external movements, T'ai Chi Ch'uan regulates breathing and causes
more oxygen to enter the bloodstream. This breathing is
more than a simple matter of inhaling and exhaling. It involves the circulation of the *ch'i*, an inner energy or life
force that directs and accelerates the free flow of oxygenated blood to all parts of the body, thus preventing stagnation. If stagnation is already present it can gradually be
eliminated. On the other hand, exercise that is too strenu-

ous could have a negative effect, increasing stagnation by
. . .

To show more clearly how the outer movements of T'ai
Chi Ch'uan harmonize with the inner energy and blood circulation, I have provided a detailed description of the flow
of the *ch'i*, as one movement sequence flows into another
throughout the form. I have also included a series of forty
diagrams to show how the outer movement facilitates the
inner flow.

In Chapter Three I discussed the beneficial effects of T'ai
Chi Ch'uan on the circulatory system and on the blood cells
in particular. Modern science now recognizes the relationship between blood cells and the immune system and its
ability to prevent and combat many serious diseases, cancer
included. The immune system fights off infection, destroying harmful bacteria, viruses, and even cancer cells. Because of its important function in maintaining health, there
continues to be a great deal of research on the preservation
and strengthening of the immune system. A recent research report on the effect of exercise showed that when
tests were performed on the blood of a group of healthy
volunteers, those who were trained in T'ai Chi Ch'uan had
a higher count of T-lymphocytes, called the "samurai of the
immune system."[1] Volunteers also had blood tests before
and after performing the T'ai Chi Ch'uan movements, and
it was found that even twenty minutes of T'ai Chi Ch'uan
exercise increased the level of T-lymphocytes, or T-cells, by
13 percent.

Those wishing to use T'ai Chi Ch'uan for the prevention
and treatment of cancer should study under a good teacher
and learn to practice the form correctly. The movements
should be done slowly and evenly, one flowing into the next
in one continuous process. The whole body should move together, arm with foot; head, shoulders, and trunk united
like one machine. An important requirement is that it be

162	The Tao of Longevity

practiced diligently and without interruption, with serious concentration, at least three or four times a day.

Focusing one's mind on the correct performance of the movements, enabling the *ch'i* to circulate and bring about healing, is perhaps the most difficult part of the exercises. Many students come to my class still thinking about their families or their work, and they cannot practice correctly. Or, they stop coming because they are busy or have lost interest. Even some seriously ill patients fail to continue to practice regularly. One of my students, David Sheinkin, a medical doctor, brought some of his cancer patients to study T'ai Chi Ch'uan with me, to aid the treatment of their cancer. The first month they came regularly and on time; then they began coming late or missing sessions altogether. I told them they should come and practice seriously because it would help cure their disease, but they said they had many things to do for their families and it was difficult to come regularly. Later on, they didn't come at all. I don't know how they are doing.

T'AI CHI CH'UAN AND CARDIOVASCULAR DISEASE

The concept of stagnation or stoppage is also important in a discussion of cardiovascular problems. In this case it is the coronary arteries that become narrowed or even blocked by fatty deposits called plaques. When the heart no longer receives sufficient quantities of oxygenated blood to function properly, heart disease develops. All the major types of heart disease—angina, cardiac arrhythmias, congestive heart failure, and myocardial infarction—are related to the failure of the blood to circulate freely. Unfortunately, the clogging of the arteries is an insidious process: by the time symptoms become apparent the coronary arteries may be 90 percent blocked. It has now been well established in the medical literature that exercise is an essential element in both the prevention and treatment of heart disease. Well-known treatment and rehabilitation centers, such as the Pritikin Centers, consider exercise to be an important aspect of their regimen.

T'ai Chi Ch'uan exercise has long been recognized in Chinese medicine as effective in both preventing and curing the arterial congestion that brings about heart disease. Y. T. Liu, in his book, *T'ai Chi Ch'uan Health Exercises for Advanced Pupils*, states that he suffered from "enlargement of the heart, hardening of arteries, and irregular pulsations." Then he began to learn T'ai Chi Ch'uan and practiced daily. He says, "After the first year the ailments were found to have been medically arrested, and after another year my heart condition was medically found to have become normal." Later Y. T. Liu became a T'ai Chi Ch'uan master. He died on the West Coast of the United States at the age of 93.

What I said earlier about the importance of learning T'ai Chi Ch'uan under a good teacher is also very important in the cure of heart disease and in the prevention of atherosclerosis. Practice should be performed daily and without interruption. Concentrating the mind on the correct performance of the form enables the *ch'i* to circulate so that accumulated impurities can be carried away and further accumulation can be prevented.

Strokes are related to stagnation, or restriction, of the blood flow as well. The blood brings oxygen and other essential elements to the brain; when the supply is interrupted, a stroke occurs. When the *ch'i* is strong, the blood circulation is strong and atherosclerosis and high blood pressure, which bring about most strokes, are prevented. Exercise also improves the blood's ability to dissolve clots, which are involved in many strokes. Because T'ai Chi Ch'uan both promotes the constant flow of oxygenated blood to the brain and enhances the blood's ability to dissolve clots, it is useful in both stroke prevention and rehabilitation.

In a previous chapter I described how T'ai Chi Ch'uan strengthens all inner systems, such as the nervous system, digestive system, respiratory system, and circulatory system. I then showed how these principles are related to the glands of the endocrine system. If the exercises are done carefully every day without interruption, they are good for the whole body, both inside and outside—even for the blood vessels, which can increase saliva and sperm. For example, when I do the T'ai Chi Ch'uan movements my mouth becomes very moist. People who dine with me in a restaurant or in my apartment see that I never need to drink water because T'ai Chi Ch'uan makes the water within circulate.

These exercises not only prevent and cure disease; they also increase the life span. For example, Master Cheng Man-Ching mentioned in his book, *Master Cheng's Thirteen Chapters on T'ai Chi Ch'uan*, that he had suffered from tuberculosis and could not be cured by medicine. He began to study T'ai Chi Ch'uan and wrote that his condition improved and his symptoms disappeared after a few months of practice. He continued to practice, not only to prevent a recurrence of tuberculosis, but also as a preventive measure against other diseases. Later on he became a famous teacher and taught both in China and America. He died at age 73. I have already mentioned Y. T. Liu, who was able to cure his heart disease through the regular performance of T'ai Chi Ch'uan, and who later became a Master. I knew both these Masters personally and know it to be true that T'ai Chi Ch'uan can cure sickness of the lungs and heart. Furthermore, in Yearning K. Chen's book, *T'ai Chi Ch'uan: Its Effects and Practical Applications*, he states,

"People suffering from neurasthenia, high blood pressure, tuberculosis, gastric and enteric diseases, paralysis, kidney diseases, etc. can all profit by the practice. Extraordinary results will come to people, even those with incurable diseases" (p. 117).

In my own experience, too, I have found that this exercise can cure some allegedly incurable diseases. One of my students had a liver disease, and I introduced him to Dr. Chia Lin Song, a Chinese medical doctor whom I mentioned in Chapter 8. He used acupuncture and moxa and prescribed pills, but they did not seem to have any effect. This student continued to practice T'ai Chi Ch'uan and now, after many years, his liver disease is gone. He has been coming to my class for almost twenty years and has not been ill again. He now has three children and lives a very happy life.

T'ai Chi Ch'uan can also cure menstrual pain. One of my students, Rosemary Birardi, suffered from severe menstrual cramps, at times so painful that she lay on the ground with tears in her eyes. After a year's practice her ailment was gone. Formerly her face was always pale; now it is sanguine and healthy. (She appears in photos 94–98.) T'ai Chi Ch'uan also cures stomach disorders and constipation. It not only prevents and cures diseases of the inner organs; it can also cure physical injuries of the body. One of my students, Joseph Guida, suffered from chronic backache and pains in the shoulder from a spinal dislocation. After two and a half years of daily practice and attending my classes, his pain is gone.

In one of two chapters added to the second edition of my book *T'ai Chi Ch'uan and I Ching* (Harper & Row, 1986), I translated and commented on the T'ai Chi Ch'uan classics. I quoted Master Chang San Feng, author of one of the outstanding classics, who said, "The *ch'i* (breath) should be concentrated and hidden within." I also quoted from *The*

Principle of the Thirteen Postures, which says, "Use the mind, concentrated, calm and quiet, to direct the *ch'i*, letting it sink down into the abdomen. It can penetrate to the bones." This means it is possible to concentrate your mind and direct the *ch'i*, which not only flows in your body but also penetrates into the bones and becomes marrow, making the bones solid and flexible. This shows that T'ai Chi Ch'uan is more important for strengthening the *ch'i* on the inside than for developing outside muscle strength. The *ch'i*, like steam or gas, can move inside and penetrate every part of the body, down to the cells.

T'AI CHI CH'UAN MOVEMENTS FOR MEDITATION AND EXERCISE

The T'ai Chi Ch'uan sequences for exercise and for meditation are very similar. For example, in meditation the circulation of *ch'i* starts small, with the Lesser Heavenly Circulation, and gradually develops to become the Grand Heavenly Circulation. First we will discuss the Beginning of the T'ai Chi Ch'uan, which relates to the Lesser Heavenly Circulation of meditation.

BEGINNING OF THE T'AI CHI CH'UAN

You should first stand and relax for several moments while you clear your mind of all thoughts; then you will be ready to start the exercise with the first movements, the Beginning of the T'ai Chi Ch'uan. As you stand erect with your arms hanging loosely at your sides and knees slightly bent (*Figures 1 and 2*), slowly breathe in and raise your hands to shoulder level. As you exhale, slowly lower your hands to the original position and bend your knees a little more, always keeping the spine erect. This movement of the arms raises the *ch'i* from its original position in the *tan t'ien* up to the navel and back down to the *tan t'ien*. In the terminology of meditation, this process is sometimes called the union of *K'an* and *Li*. *K'an*, representing water and the kidneys, also refers to the region of the lower abdomen, where the *tan t'ien* is located. *Li*, which represents fire and the heart, designates the heart center. Thus the Beginning of the T'ai Chi Ch'uan circulates the *ch'i* between these two vital centers. In meditation the air (postnatal breathing[2]) comes from the nostrils and sinks down to the navel. The *ch'i* (prenatal breathing) comes from the *tan t'ien* and rises to the navel. You may wish to repeat this movement several times before continuing on to Grasp Bird's Tail, which stabilizes the *ch'i* in the *tan t'ien* as the right hand passes downward alongside the body (*Figure 3*). When the *ch'i* has stabilized, both the mind and breath are concentrated in the abdomen. In Taoist terminology this is referred to as "Fire Dwells in the Water Place." Thus the abdomen is called a "stove" in meditation and is capable of boiling water, which is abundant here, and turning it into steam. This causes the water to recirculate through the body. It can prevent and cure diseases in which too much fluid is retained in the abdomen tissues, such as inflammation of the bladder. It is also an integral part of the refinement of *jing* (sperm) into *ch'i* (energy).

The next sequence begins with the Push Up and continues to move the *ch'i* in the Lesser Heavenly Circulation. Turn to the right (*Figure 4*) and move your right hand straight up in front of your body, bringing the *ch'i* from the abdomen to the navel (*Figure 5*). Then execute Pull Back (*Figures 6, 7, 8*), concentrating your thoughts and breathing on the motion of the left hand, which guides the *ch'i* from the navel back to the abdomen. The left hand circles around and meets the right, palm to palm at chest level

(*Figure 9*). This sequence is called "Press Forward" and again guides the *ch'i* from the abdomen to the navel. Now sit back and separate your hands (*Figure 10*); the *ch'i* returns to the abdomen by following the motion of the body as it sits back. The next sequence is Push Forward (*Figure 11*), which sends the *ch'i* once more to the navel. You may repeat it one or more times from Push Up or even from the Beginning of the T'ai Chi Ch'uan to achieve the Lesser Heavenly Circulation. Then you may continue with Turn Body and Single Whip (*Figures 12 and 13*). Turn Body is the turning point at which you begin a new process: the Grand Heavenly Circulation.

This process begins after the Single Whip, in which you extend your arms to each side, forming a half circle (*Figure 14*). The right leg is extended toward the corner, and in this open position the *ch'i* penetrates the whole body. With your weight balanced over the left leg, move both arms and the right leg toward the center in the sequence Play Guitar Right (*Figure 15*). The left palm is opposite the right elbow and the right leg rests lightly on the heel. The *ch'i* becomes concentrated along the *Jen Mo* (front of the body).

THE GRAND HEAVENLY CIRCULATION

In the Grand Heavenly Circulation of the T'ai Chi Ch'uan this same movement of *ch'i*—first opening and spreading to the whole body and then closing and concentrating along the *Jen Mo*—is achieved in the sequences Slant Flying and Play Guitar Right (see pp. 80 and 81).

The sequence continues after Play Guitar Right with Pull Back (*Figure 16*), Step Forward, and Strike With Shoulder (*Figure 17*), which constitute a conjunction joining the Lesser and Grand Heavenly Circulations. The Grand Heavenly Circulation actually begins with the form White Crane Spreads Wings (*Figure 18*). In this sequence the weight is balanced on the right foot and the right hand moves up to the front of the head. This upward movement of the hand guides the *ch'i* from the lower abdomen to the forehead, along the Channel of Function, or *Jen Mo*. As the sequence continues, the right knee bends lower, the right hand drops, and the trunk of the body rotates to the right (*Figure 19*). These coordinated movements guide the *ch'i* downward again along the *Jen Mo* from the forehead down to the lower abdomen. Then, just before the end of the rotation to the right, the right hand moves slightly behind the back. The purpose of this movement is to guide the *ch'i* from the lower abdomen through the pubic region and back to the base of the spine. The sequence continues with a step of the left foot, and then as weight is shifted to the left, the left arm brushes past the left knee and the right arm circles back and around, passing by the ear to push forward. This sequence, called "Brush Knee and Push," guides the *ch'i* up the Channel of Control, or *Tu Mo*, from the base of the spinal column to the crown of the head (*Figure 20*). Play Guitar Left, Step Forward and Punch, Draw Back and Push Forward, turn your body to the front, Cross Hands. This is the end of the first section. (Additional T'ai Chi Ch'uan movements for meditation can be found in my earlier book *T'ai Chi Ch'uan and Meditation*, Chapter 10.)

The mental concentration that directs the *ch'i* is also part of meditation. The sequences of T'ai Chi Ch'uan movements which facilitate the flow of *ch'i* through the body are almost the same when used as exercise and as meditation. So far I have emphasized their use as exercise to prevent or cure stagnation and its related diseases. Now I will deal with their use in the relief of stress-related conditions.

In China meditation has been known since ancient times as a means to achieve bodily health. We have the words of Lao Tzu, "Who can [make] the muddy water [clear]? Let it be still, and it will gradually become clear. Who can secure the condition of rest? Let movement go on, and the condition of rest will gradually arise." As quoted in the Preface to this edition we have the even earlier words (2697 B.C.) of Hwang Ti, the Yellow Emperor: "There is nothing to be seen, nothing to be heard. Hold your spirit in stillness; your body becomes correct (healthy) . . ."

Health exercises have been associated with meditation since prehistoric times. In Taoist philosophy there is a complex, complementary relationship between movement, as practiced in T'ai Chi Ch'uan, and the state of rest and inner peace that is the goal of meditation. Taoist meditation combines movement, breathing, and mental concentration. The T'ai Chi Ch'uan practitioner works to develop a peaceful state of mind through breathing that is directed by externally visible movement. If all of these elements are harmonized correctly, T'ai Chi Ch'uan can be even more effective than sitting meditation.

In speaking of "correct" performance of T'ai Chi Ch'uan, I am not urging the accomplishment of a form that can be admired by observers. In correct performance all muscles are soft and relaxed. The mind is clear of outside stimuli and is able to concentrate fully on the strong inner flow of the *ch'i*. The result is a release from harmful tension and stress.

Meditation, by relieving stress, increases our natural inner power potential and immune system, enabling the body to fend off and conquer disease. Anxiety and disease feed each other: anxiety makes the body vulnerable to disease, and worrying about one's illness creates further anxiety. Meditation is a way of purifying this stagnation of the mind.

In the years that I have researched the relationship between T'ai Chi Ch'uan and meditation I have found much evidence that the many movements that enhance the flow of ch'i through the body also relieve anxiety and thus prevent and alleviate disease. The importance of stress control is amply demonstrated by medical research. Especially notable was a study reported some years ago by Dr. Herbert Benson and his colleagues at Harvard University. They found that regular meditation, which induces relaxation, could actually lower blood pressure. In his book, *The Relaxation Response*,[3] Dr. Benson describes meditation as a new approach to prevent and treat disease, and says, "Because our world is changing at an ever-increasing pace, time for meditation should be recognized by society as an essential part of daily life."

More recently, a comprehensive treatment for heart disease was studied and is now being proposed for wider use. As reported in the November 14, 1989, The New York *Times* and in the May 1990 issue of *Prevention Magazine*, Dr. Dean Ornish calls for an entirely new life-style that includes the two crucial ingredients: namely, meditation and proper breathing. Heart patients should include another ingredient—visualizing the reduction of blockage taking place in the arteries, a process that is suggestive of the mental concentration on the flow of the *ch'i*, an essential element in T'ai Chi Ch'uan. Moderate exercise and diet control are also essential elements in the program. Not only do these life-style changes reduce plaque buildup, but an actual unclogging of the coronary arteries has been demonstrated. Dr. Ornish said, "One of the most significant changes was the reduction in stenosis, or the narrowing of the arteries. In heart disease, fatty deposits accumulate in the blood vessels, clogging the channel the blood passes through. The narrowing can also foster the formation of clots, which block the blood flow, thus destroying the heart muscle."[4]

T'ai Chi Ch'uan has, for many centuries, offered the benefits of stress reduction through meditation, gentle exercise, and concentration of the mind on the free flow of the *ch'i*. It is reassuring to find that the benefits are now being reaffirmed by medical science. Nutrition has also long been a concern of Chinese medicine. In the next chapter I will discuss nutrition in the prevention and control of disease.

NOTES

1. "Reverse Health Disease Naturally," *Prevention*, May 1990.

2. A Taoist concept. The comingling of "postnatal" (regular) and "prenatal" (fetal) breathing occurs in Taoist deep breathing technique.

3. Herbert Benson, and Miriam Z. Klipper, *The Relaxation Response*, New York: Avon, 1976.

4. Daniel Coleman, "Life-Style Shift Can Unclog Ailing Arteries, Study Finds," The New York *Times*, November 14, 1989.

CHAPTER 10
FOOD AS MEDICINE

In the last chapter I referred to the value of exercise and meditation in the prevention and cure of cancer and other major diseases. Chinese doctors have also used food, herbs, and certain medicines to make prevention and treatment more effective.

Traditional Chinese doctors, in contrast to Western doctors, have always advised their patients on which foods to eat and which to avoid. They have believed since ancient times that food and herbs can prevent and cure disease. Any or all parts of a plant or herb may be used: roots, stems, leaves, flowers, seeds, and peel. For many years Western medical authorities scoffed at these ancient remedies, but in the last few decades modern pharmaceutical science has rediscovered many of them.

The first Chinese medical encyclopedia, *Pen-tsao Kang-mu*, which was used in the Sung dynasty (A.D. 960–1276), listed the medicinal plants in use at that time. Among those listed was Ma Huang, meaning "yellow astringent." From the twigs of this plant a tea was made to treat asthma and other respiratory ailments, to improve the blood circulation, to reduce fevers, and to improve urinary functioning. In the nineteenth century Japanese scientists discovered that it contained ephedrine.[1] In 1923 two American-trained scientists, Carl F. Schmidt and K. K. Chen, who had heard

of its many uses while on a trip to China, further researched this drug. Ephedrine is now widely used in Western medicine as a nerve and heart stimulant and to alleviate
asthma.

Another plant long valued in China for its health-giving
properties is the lily. It was mentioned in *The Book of
Odes*, one of the five classics of Confucius, where it was
described as the "flower to dispel worry." In the Chinese
magazine *Sinorama*[2] I found an informative article on the
lily as medicine. It mentions that the lily was also listed in
the *Pen-tsao Kang-mu* encyclopedia and that it was said to
cure fevers, aid urination, and clear the intestines. The ancients ate the boiled bulb, but today the bud, just before it
opens into a blossom, is more often used. It is called
"golden needle" and is considered delicious.

Another article reports, "The lily was also purported to
increase a woman's chance of having a male baby, should
she wear it or consume it. In the Ming dynasty (1368–1662)
they were planted all around the palace to enhance the
chances of a son being born to the emperor."[3] It seems that
lilies are efficacious in many ways, both mental and physical!

Recent analysis of the lily's properties by Li Chin-fung,
of the Graduate Institute of Food Science and Technology
at National Taiwan University, has shown it to be rich in
Vitamin C and minerals. A traditional Chinese doctor, Dr.
Chiu, verified the use of the lily to cure cancer. He says the
lily has a very strong power to diminish any poison and to
reduce fever. It works effectively to cure cancer without
adding another poison. The lily is also recognized by the
Chinese herb authority, Professor Kan Wei Soon, and his
assistant, Dr. Tsa Chi Yung, a medical doctor from America.

I collect reports of both Western and Chinese research
on the use of food and herbs in the treatment of cancer.

Especially important is the work of Dr. William F. C. Chao, who for thirty years specialized in the diagnosis and treatment of cancer. He was a pioneer in combining traditional methods with modern scientific understanding and treated patients in many Asian countries and in America. I was acquainted with Dr. Chao for about twenty years and knew him to be highly professional.

Dr. Chao introduced his book, *Chinese Cancer Therapy*, by saying that Chinese medicine is the result of much accumulated experience, beginning with Emperor Shen Nung (2838 B.C.), who tasted many healing drugs, Emperor Huang Ti (2698–2598 B.C.), and the writing of *Nei Ching* (the *Canon of Internal Medicine*). He stated that the goal of Chinese cancer treatment is the internal dissipation of cancer cells without the use of toxic elements, in contrast to Western practices of surgical excision and destruction by radiation and chemotherapy.

Diet was an important part of Dr. Chao's treatment. Some foods were considered nutritious for the cancer patient and others were considered undesirable, as they appeared to nourish the cancer cells and make them grow.[4] He stressed the need for highly nutritious foods, rich in vitamins and minerals according to modern nutritional standards, and emphasized the use of vegetables and fruits. Among the foods forbidden to the cancer patient was seafood. His book provides many examples of patients who were almost cured but who then ate fish and had the cancer return. In my own experience, seafood has caused a troublesome itching of the skin. For a long time I ate no seafood. Now, when I eat a small amount of seafood, such as crab or shrimp, the itching returns. Dr. Chao also used Chinese herbs and medicines, after analyzing their properties, and found them to be effective in preventing and curing cancer.

Dr. Chao was criticized by Western-trained medical doctors, but he nevertheless has many documented cures. Two of my students were treated by him. The first, a man named Reggie Jackson, was diagnosed by American doctors as having a malignant tumor in his chest. After treatment with herbs and a vegetarian diet, his tumor disappeared and there was no need for an operation. Today he is in very good health. Another student, Noa Notham, received a gunshot wound that was not serious in itself, but which later developed into a tumor suspected of being cancerous. I introduced her to Dr. Chao, who diagnosed the tumor as incipient cancer. He asked her about her family and found that her father had cancer of the tongue. He decided to first strengthen her body so that she could receive the full benefit of the medicine he prescribed. He suggested she eat a soup made of a special kind of bird's nest that is built by swallows who live by the sea. They eat fish and use the fish and their own saliva to build nests in the rocks. This is considered a nutritious food in China. After a few weeks her body weight had increased five pounds. Then Dr. Chao gave her special pills. She also practiced T'ai Chi Ch'uan more diligently than before. After several months the tumor disappeared. Dr. Chao calls this use of a variety of treatments "interlocking treatment." It includes eating nutritious food, avoiding other foods that can strengthen the cancer, Chinese medicine, and exercise.

Medical literature is full of reports authenticating the value of food in the prevention and treatment of cancer, cardiovascular disease, and many other illnesses. New scientific research is aimed at a more precise understanding of the metabolic processes and the reactions of enzymes, which make some foods potent cancer preventatives. The New York *Times* recently reported one such research project. Dr. Chang S. Yang, who was born in China but received his advanced science degrees at Cornell University, is a cancer researcher at Rutgers University's College of

Pharmacy. His work is supported by the National Institutes of Health and the American Institute of Cancer Research. His goal is to prove or disprove past concepts of diet and disease. He reports that so far his research supports the belief that a balanced diet, with plenty of vegetables and fruits, inhibits the formation of certain cancers.

Dr. Yang is also associated with a large-scale project in Northern China, in a region with a very high incidence of cancer. The causes, he says, appear to be a diet low in nutrition, the use of Chinese pickled vegetables, and water containing carcinogens. To test the effectiveness of nutritional supplements, half of the 30,000 inhabitants in the study are being given vitamins and minerals and half are being given placebos. Dr. Yang is also finding, as did Dr. Chao, that at some stages of cancer, otherwise desirable foods may promote the growth of cancer cells; Dr. Chao also mentioned that Chinese pickled vegetables should be avoided. In a recent article Dr. Yang said, "a balanced diet—moderation and just enjoying the vegetables—is probably the best policy."[5]

Moderation is an important theme in Chinese philosophy. In the writings of Confucius and in Taoist literature the doctrine of the middle way is emphasized. Confucius took pleasure in good food but he enjoyed it in moderation. Dr. Chao, in *Chinese Cancer Therapy*, said that although too little nutritious food could cause disease, "excessive nutrition or hormones can also cause cancer, thus going to the extreme either way will cause imbalance." Now scientific research is finding that moderation in the amount of food eaten promotes health and longevity.[6] Among the researchers reporting their findings are Dr. Roy L. Walford of the University of California in Los Angeles, a pioneer in the study of calorie-restricted diets, Dr. Edward Masoro of the University of Texas, who has studied longevity in rodents, and Dr. Byung Pal Yu of the same university, who has studied the role of oxygen in aging. Once again an ancient Chinese health belief is finding scientific support.

Much important research on diet and disease is now being conducted in China, due in part to Chinese medicine's long-standing interest in the subject and the fact that China provides an excellent laboratory: regional populations tend to be stable in terms of genetic makeup, crops raised, and diet consumed. In one project, scientists at the Beijing Cancer Institute studied mortality in 24 provinces and found a correlation between low selenium content in local food products and a high incidence of cancer.[7] Selenium is known to strengthen the immune system and help the body resist cancer.

In a reported New York *Times* article, Jane Brody reported on another study being conducted in China. The article states, "Early findings from the most comprehensive large study ever undertaken on the relationship between diet and the risk of developing disease are challenging much of the American dietary dogma. The study . . . paints a bold portrait of a plant-based eating plan that is more likely to promote health than disease.[7] The headline for the article, "Huge Study of Diet Indicts Fat and Meat," speaks for itself. The research is so extensive, "covering the whole diet panoply as it relates to disease," Brody said, that it will continue to provide information for many years to come, but it is now apparent, however, that vegetables again rate as highly desirable food.

The Chinese study started with the goal of exploring the dietary causes of cancer, but it has since been expanded to include metabolic, infectious, and heart disease. In affluent regions, where the inhabitants can afford more red meat, heart disease, diabetes, and cancer, "the diseases of affluence," are more prevalent. Additional data on the relation between cholesterol levels and disease are being compiled, and opinions on desirable amounts of fat are being revised.

Jane Brody reports, "Reducing dietary fat to less than 30 percent of calories, as is currently recommended for Americans, may not be enough to curb the risk of heart disease and cancer. To make a significant impact, the Chinese data imply, a maximum of 20 percent of calories from fat—and preferably only 10 to 15 percent—should be consumed."[9]

In summary, the ancient belief of Chinese medicine that food and edible herbs could prevent and cure diseases such as cancer and heart disease is now being fully substantiated by the advanced methods of modern science. Good nutrition is part of a way of life that includes proper exercise to promote the circulation of the *ch'i*, or vital energy, and meditation to bring about inner peace.

I will discuss several Chinese health foods in the next chapter.

NOTES

1. *Magic and Medicine of Plants*, Reader's Digest Association, Pleasantville, New York, 1986.

2. *Sinorama*, December, 1988.

3. *Sinorama*, April 1975.

4. Chart of diet for patients from *Chinese Cancer Therapy*, William F. C. Chao (Taipei, 1965).

5. The New York *Times*, April 29, 1990, New Jersey edition.

6. The New York *Times*, *Science Times*, April 17, 1990.

7. Mark F. McCarthy, *Health Benefits of Supplemental Nutrition*, 2nd ed. (Nutriguard Research, 1988).

8. Jane Brody, "Huge Study of Diet Indicts Fat and Meat," The New York *Times*, May 8, 1990.

9. Ibid.

CHAPTER 11:
CHINESE HEALTH FOOD

Mencius says, "If you have nutrition, everything will experience growth; without nutrition everything perishes." Different kinds of nutrition can affect mental and physical life. Creatures like the horse and cow that eat grass have great strength, but little intelligence. Meat eaters such as the lion, tiger, and birds of prey like the eagle have even greater strength but are also easier to anger. The appearance of food also has its effects. Animals that have hair like grass eat grass. Birds eat the leaves or fruits of trees and their feathers are of the same shape as the leaves. Man eats with more complexity, ingesting flesh, grains, vegetables, fruits, making him strong and intelligent.

TAOIST MEDICINE AND NUTRITION

Most enlightened Taoists are also physicians and herbalists. They learned how to cure and prevent sickness and increase health and promote longevity. They believed eating the proper foods can cure and prevent disease, eliminating the necessity of taking medicine.

The legendary king Shen Nung, the Divine Husband-

man, who reigned from 2757 to 2697 B.C., experimented
with all the plants, analyzed them by taste, color, and quality, and discovered their usage. It is said that when the
clan of Pao Hsi, the legendary king, was gone, there sprang
up the clan of the Divine Husbandman. He split a piece of
wood for the plowshare and bent a piece of wood for the
plow handle and taught the world the advantage of laying
open the earth with a plow. He probably took this idea from
the hexagram *I* that means increase.

Through the years each generation had its sages and
medical doctors. The most remarkable physician and herbalist, Sun Ssu Mo, lived 101 years, from A.D. 581 to 682.
Several emperors wished to make him an important medical official, but he declined the offer, thinking that research
and aid to the poor would better serve the royal family. He
contributed many devices that greatly helped mankind.
The emperor gave him the title "The King of Remedies and
God of Medicine." Even today he is still respected by the
Chinese people. Just a few years ago, for example, both the
People's Republic of China and Nationalist China cele-
brated his contribution to the prevention of smallpox by
issuing a stamp in his honor.

It is said that when Sun Ssu Mo began his career as a
physician, in his birthplace in northwest China, now called
Shensi Province, he had few patients. This was because he
had learned the art by himself, not from an expert practitioner, and did not come from a family of physicians. Only
those close to death would go to him as a last resort, and
they would die before the diagnosis was completed. People
were reluctant to trust him. When he realized there was no
hope of making his living in his birthplace, he sought his
fortune elsewhere.

He met a fortune teller and asked him where he could go
for a better fortune. The fortune teller told him his fortune
would be in the South, and when his wife's shoes would

weigh around ten pounds, he would begin to have great fame and fortune.

So he and his wife traveled south and crossed the Yangtze River, which has a very wet climate, especially during the month of June, when nearly everyday it rains all day. They walked on the muddy road, and his wife felt very tired and asked to rest because her shoes were heavy and full of mud. Sun Ssu Mo remembered the words of the fortune teller, and so they rested under a willow tree. They saw some people carrying a coffin from which dripped several drops of blood. Sun Ssu Mo said, "Whoever is in the coffin is still alive, for if there were death, there could be no blood." They told him the woman in the coffin could not give birth and so had died. He opened the coffin and put an acupuncture needle on the area over the woman's heart. Her infant cried, was born, and the woman heaved a long sigh and opened her eyes. This is the Chinese story of how one needle saved two lives. From that time on, Sun Ssu Mo's fame grew and spread.

Sun Ssu Mo retreated into the mountains and, in his later years, wrote several books. One is called *A Thousand Ounces of Gold Prescriptions*. In this book he says when the illness is discovered, it should first be treated by food; only when food fails, should medicine be prescribed. Western nutrition is based upon the same concept of prevention of illness through proper diet.

BARLEY

Many different types of food, easy to acquire at a reasonable price, have great nutritional and remedial qualities, and can be found world-wide. For example, pearl barley can be found everywhere and is about fifty cents a pound in American supermarkets.

The ancients knew the value of pearl barley. In the Eastern Han dynasty, A.D. 25–147, there was a general, Ma Yuan, who conquered Vietnam. Because Ma Yuan's birthplace was northwest China, he was not accustomed to the Vietnamese climate, which was wetter than his native land and caused him to be sick. He ate barley to cure his rheumatism and make himself calmer inside and healthier outside. Ma Yuan realized the barley produced in Vietnam is bigger than that grown in other parts of China, and when he returned victoriously to China he carried several wagons of barley. The emperor gave him the title of Fu Po Chiang Chun, which literally means "General That Conquered Waves," because Vietnam is close to the sea. His fellow officers were jealous of him and slandered Ma Yuan, saying he took many pearls as bribes from Vietnam. This was refuted easily when it was shown that Vietnamese barley looked like pearls.

Many present-day governments spend millions of dollars on research to cure cancer. A Nationalist Chinese medical doctor, William Chao, uses barley to cure cancer. In his book *How to Cure Cancer*, he says, "Of course there are different causes and types of cancer that require the use of various Chinese medicines for cure; however barley is an important element in the remedy." On page 162, he describes barley: "The taste is lightly sweet. The function is to aid the urine and increase the body's health. It can help the cancer patient if his digestion is weak and he lacks nutrition. If his foot swells, use 10 to 20 grams."

In Japan Dr. Yashihica has lectured on Chinese medical science's contributions toward the cure of cancer. One prescription used barley, water chestnuts, Ho-Tze (an astringent nut used for toothache and as a stomachic), and Ting Liu Ah (a kind of climbing plant), each ten grams twice a day. The Japanese call the mixture WTTC. Also produced in Taiwan by the Shun T'ien T'ang company, it is said to cure stomach ache and cancer. An experiment showed that after three months, of 168 people taking the medicine, thirty-six percent had substantially recovered and twenty-one percent were completely cured. In 1948, the International Cancer Research Annual Meeting recognized that pearl barley can cure and prevent cancer.

The ancient Chinese book *Four Divine Foods* used barley, *Pachyma Cocos*, yams, and the seeds of the water lily cooked with rice to prevent and cure cancer. This prescription comes from the Taoist book *Eating for Nutrition*.

If you want to simplify this, soak about ten grams of pearl barley in warm water approximately two hours until soft, add about one-fourth pound rice and cook. A gruel results if a lot of water is used; if less is used, the result is more like regular rice. Either way, the mixture is used to prevent rheumatism, nourish inner energy, and benefit the stomach and digestion.

Pearl barley can be prepared with chicken in this manner:

> 1 cleaned 2- or 3-lb. chicken
> 6 grams pearl barley
> 1.5 grams *Cnidium Officinale*
> 3 grams salted pulpy mushrooms

Cut chicken into pieces and put with above ingredients into a pot of boiling water. Return to boil. Then cover pot and simmer for about two hours. Add salt, wine, vegetables, such as celery, carrots, and onions, and ginger; simmer till vegetables are cooked through. The soup alone is good for arthritis.

WATER MEALS

RICE

The Chinese cook rice in two different ways. One is the usual cooked rice eaten in Chinese restaurants. Another kind, called Shi-Fan (water meal or water rice), uses much more water. It is cooked approximately 40 minutes, first under a strong fire until the water boils, then simmered under a low flame, adding water as needed. The rice retains its wholesome shape. The Chinese eat it mostly for breakfast and at midnight snacks. Easy to digest and nourishing to the intestines, it is especially good for the aged and sick or for children who lack milk. It can be mixed with regular rice or cooked with another kind of grain without rice and even cooked with vegetables, meat, chicken, or fish. For medical purposes, it can be mixed with various herbs. Listed below are some water meals and their possible effects.

GRAIN WATER MEALS

Wheat: Cooling, thrist-quenching, used in fever cases.
Glutinous Rice: Used as a demulcent in diarrhea and vomiting and as a local application for smallpox in children.
Ordinary Rice: Diuretic, thirst relieving, and nutritious.
Red Beans: Diuretic, curative in gout, resolvant in dropsy.
Green Beans: Thirst relieving and cooling.
Browned Flour: (wheat flour fried or baked until brown): Used to cure "white dysentery."
Barley Kernels: Beneficial to digestive organs and curative in rheumatism.

NUT OR SEED WATER MEALS

Lotus Seed: Astringent in diarrhea and dysentery; strengthens spleen and stomach.

Water Lily Seed (Euryate Ferox): Constrictive and tonic; improves hearing and vision.

Water Chestnut: Cooling to viscera, beneficial to digestive organs.

Chestnut: Strengthens loins and legs; tonic to kidneys.

Apricot Kernel: Composed of peach or apricot kernels and certain flowers; used for coughs; as calmative and stomachic.

Poppy Seeds: Benefits large intestine; thirst relieving.

Pine-Nut Kernel: Moistens lungs and heart and harmonizes large intestine.

Black Pepper, Boymia Rutoecarpa, Smart Weed, Hemp Seed: All carminatives, used individually to treat bowel pain.

Sesame Seed, Kernel of Prunes Japonica: Helps cure rheumatism and moistens intestines.

Seed of Perilla Ocymoides: Carminative and strengthening to diaphragm.

VEGETABLE WATER MEALS

Radish: Digestive; beneficial to diaphragm.

Carrot: Peptic, carminative.

Purslane: Used for swelling and rheumatism.

Rape: Harmonizing to centers (inner organs); carminative.

Pond Weed: Beneficial to stomach and spleen.

Spinach: Moistens and harmonizes viscera.

Shepherd's Purse: Benefits liver and brightens eye.

Celery: Cooling and beneficial to intestines.

Mallow: Moistening in feverishness; peptic.

Mustard: Prevents effluvia and expels phlegm.

Leek: Warming to viscera.

Rehmannia Glutinosa: Prepared by boiling the root with rice; when it's nearly done, add curds, honey, and boil dry. Afterward, boil the mixture in water. Eaten as a tonic to the blood and as a general constructive.

*Potato:*Strengthens kidneys, digestive organs, and virile organs.
Taro: Considered highly nutritious.
Flour of Lily Bulb: Harmonizing to inner organs; moistening to lungs.
Wild Jujube: Strengthens gall and alleviates fever.
Lycium Sinsense: Beneficial to kidneys and blood.
Scallion Bulb: Used as cure for "cold diarrhea" in aged.
Ginger: Antiseptic and warming to viscera.
Red Pepper: Prevents colds and malaria.
Fennel: Used as cure for hernia and harmonizes stomach.
Salted Onion: Diaphoretic and lubricating to muscles.
Pachyma Cocos: Overall nutrient and tonic.
Bamboo Leaf Decoction: Purifies heart and relieves thirst.

MEAT WATER MEALS

Kidney of Pig, Deer, or Sheep: Considered to be strengthening in all diseases of kidney.
Chicken or Sheep Liver: Used in diseases of liver.
Broth of Duck, Carp, Beef, Sheep, or Chicken: Used in dropsy and to increase energy and improve overall health.
Meal with Milk: To gain weight.
Meal with Deer's-horn Glue: Eaten to benefit the vital principle, and as a constructive food.

SPICES AND VEGETABLES

The following commonly used spices and vegetables have medicinal value.

Ginger is useful both to make food tasty and as an herbal medicine. Confucius was never without ginger when he ate. It can make food more delicious but has even more value in medicinal uses: to combat colds and rheumatism, to make the blood and breath flow more easily, and to increase the heat in the body. Many Chinese prescriptions contain ginger; it helps to guide the medication to the proper point in the body. It is often used in combination with Chinese dates. Crystallized ginger can be taken after eating to aid digestion.

Garlic is used in most of the world as a food flavoring. It has a very strong taste. It can also neutralize poisons in the body, stimulate sexual energy, and fight colds and tuberculosis. *Celery* is helpful in regulating high blood pressure.

The bulb of the lily is used for food and medicine. It is beneficial to the lungs in treating coughs and asthma. It is considered to be a tonic, eliminant, and expectorant. The lily bulb also has quieting effects and can be used to treat postpartum depression. Externally it is used on swellings and ulcers.

VEGETARIAN DIET

Vegetarian food has become increasingly popular in the West, particularly among young people. Many people adhere entirely or mainly to a diet of organic vegetables and fruit, vegetable and fruit juices, and herb teas, finding that it increases their energy and makes them feel healthy without leading to undesirable weight gain. In fact, it has been found that such a diet is ideal for those who need to lose weight and restore themselves to more comfortable, healthy proportions.

In the Catskill Mountains in New York, a highly successful health resort, New Age Health Farm, which has been written about in the New York *Daily News*, *Harper's Bazaar*, and the *Village Voice*, has helped many people lose significant amounts of weight and greatly improve their health through a program of exercise, fasting, and a lacto-vegetarian diet consisting mainly of organic vegetables.

Vegetarian diet and use of herbs are also emphasized by societies devoted to the practice of T'ai Chi Ch'uan for health and longevity, such as those organized by Dr. David Sheinkin, a physician in Rockland County, New York, and by Susan De Long, a T'ai Chi Ch'uan teacher in Philadelphia.

FRUITS

Besides protein foods and vegetables, a well-balanced diet should include a good amount of fruit. Fruits are full of vitamins and minerals and help cleanse the body. The apple, both in China and the West, has a good reputation as a health food. It is widely available in all seasons at minimal expense. In China, it is used for nourishment and as a cure for diarrhea. It is beneficial to the digestive tract and can cure headaches. Topped with honey, it keeps the body in good health and adds luster and smoothness to the skin. In ancient times, Chinese Taoists would eat an apple in place of a meal.

Bananas can also be found in every season and nearly everywhere at very reasonable prices. The banana has some protein and is beneficial to the stomach and intestines. When ripe, it can help cure constipation and diarrhea. A banana eaten with sesame oil may alleviate severe constipation.

Peaches are most readily available in summer and early autumn. They are rich in vitamins. They are beneficial to the heart and the blood circulation. Overindulgence in them may result in fever. If the peach has excessive amounts of hair on its skin, one should peel it or remove the hair with rough paper. The pit inside the stone has great medicinal value—for example, it is used to cure coughing. If a woman's menstrual flow is stagnated, she should cook twenty peach seeds together with lotus root and drink the mixture. Persimmons come to the market in autumn. When picked the fruit is green but turns yellow, orange, then red as it ripens. It can be eaten fresh, or, when ripe enough, it can be juiced. It can also be sun-dried. The taste is sweet. Persimmons are used to treat fever of the lung and asthma and to relieve phlegm and coughing fits. The dry persimmon is used to benefit the stomach and spleen and nourish the lungs and intestines. Sugar obtained from the persimmon is used to cure piles, high blood pressure, and the coughing up of blood.

CHINESE TEAS

Easterners, especially the Chinese, drink tea like Westerners drink coffee. The leaves of the tea tree are best when most tender. The Chinese drink tea for enjoyment. They drink it slowly, poetically, for its taste and not merely to quench thirst. The Chinese attitude is epitomized in the famous Chinese novel Tsao Hsueh-chin's *The Dream of the Red Chamber*. Two young girls are discussing the manner of drinking tea. One says, "One cup is for enjoyment, two cups are to alleviate thirst, but three cups are called 'a donkey drinking water.'"

The Chinese have more than a thousand kinds of tea. Some teas are very expensive and differ greatly in price from others. Some Chinese are so fond of tea that they would sell their property in order to obtain it. In the T'ang Dynasty, a man named Lu Yu wrote a three-volume book called *Tza Ching* (The Classic of Tea). The first volume analyzes the different types of tea, tells about the history and sources of the tea, and gives advice on how to judge the quality. The second volume tells how to prepare the tea using spring water, snow water, rain water, or water from collecting the snow off various flowers and trees and to cook the tea over burning coals of bamboo or pine. The third volume tells about what instruments are used in the preparation of the tea, such as stoves, pots, and cups. The book was so detailed that many people called Lu Yu the God of Tea.

There are two main categories of tea: Green tea and black (red) tea. Green tea is mostly consumed in summer, black tea mostly in winter. The Mongolians and Russians drink black tea mixed with sugar and milk, the way Westerners drink coffee. The Chinese believe that the effect of the good tea upon the system is highly beneficial. It is thought to strengthen the voice, give luster to the eyes, improve the constitution and mental faculties, and cleanse the body by aiding digestion and regulating the body temperature.

The different names and brands of a tea allude to the place from which it comes, the time of the picking, and the nature of the leaf; some names are merely trademarks.

1. *P'u-erh Ch'a* (Tea) 普 洱 茶 -is produced in the P'uerh Fu District in Yunan Province between China and Burma. Yunan is a high plateau; P'uerh Fu is a mountainous dry place. There is a lake in the mountain called P'uerh-h'a where the better tea is produced. This tea has two colors, black and green. The green neutralizes poison in the digestive tract, relieves drunkeness and increases saliva. Formerly the men and women who gathered the tea pressed the leaves together into a round shape like a ball. It came in three different sizes, big, middle and small. The big size equals about six or seven pounds and is in the shape of a man's head and so is called man head tea. To make it easy to carry they put a hole in the middle and inserted a string through it. They cut pieces off with a knife. Today it is no

longer produced this way because of modern transportation. When I was young, if I caught a cold or had indigestion problems, my mother always cut this tea and cooked it
for me to drink.

2. *Lung Ching Ch'a* (Tea)___龍非___ -means tea of the
Dragon Well. Dragon Well is a place which is located in the
Hang Chow District of the Chekiang Province where good
green tea is produced. It can relieve fever and produce
saliva. During the summertime if it is accompanied by the
chrysanthemum it is more effective, more tasteful and
especially beneficial for the eyes.

3. *Shui-Sha-Lien-Ch'a* (Tea)水 沙 漣 茶 -is produced in
Formosa where the forest is so thick with bushes that the
leaves of the tea never receive sunshine. Therefore it is a
cooling tea and is used in the treatment of fevers. Also it is
used as an agitant to cause the eruption of smallpox.

Brewed tea leaves are often placed in a crock where they
remain until they change form and can be used as a
medicine. The more aged the concoction is the more beneficial it is in the treatment of external bodily wounds such as
dog-bites, old burns and bruises, ulcers, and swellings. It is
applied directly on the skin.

4. *Lung-Ch'i-Ch'a* (Tea)___龍荇茶___ -is grown in the
Kwangsi Province and is often made into brick tea. It is
used as a healant in malaria and all forms of toxemia and
also in diarrhea and dysentery.

5. *An-Hua-Ch'a* (Tea)___安化茶___ -is produced in the
An-Hua District of Hunan Province. The leaves produce a
tea dark in color which is considered to be a black tea. It
has a bittersweet taste. This tea is used like regular tea but
is valued greatly for its medicinal powers.

6. *Hsiang-T'an-Ch'a* (Tea)___湘潭茶___ -is grown in the
Hsiang-Tan District of Hunan Province. At one time it was
presented to the Emperor, Princess and high officers.

7. *Hsueh-Ch'a* (Tea)___雪茶___ -means the snow tea. It

grows in the mountains of Ling-Chiang-Fu in Yunan Province. It is found in the snow region, therefore it is called the snow tea. Samples of it are difficult to obtain therefore the price is high. This tea is held to be warming. If a glassful is taken on a bitter cold day the inner organs are heated as if a fire had been lit. Because of this it is used to cure colds and dysentery.

8. *Lo-Chieh-Ch'a* (Tea)__羅岕茶__ -is produced in the west side of Nutang Mountain and named after the man in ancient times who raised it.

Nutang Mountain is a sacred place of the Taoist religion, where many temples existed and which gave birth to the inner schools of the martial arts. It is said that Chang-San-Feng created there the T'ai Chi Ch'uan which is now popular in the whole world.

The summer solstice is the best time to harvest the tea leaves. Mountainous regions are the only place where this tea can grow, therefore it is held in high value. It's medical use is for the treatment of pulmonary troubles and dropsy.

9. *P'o-T'o-Ch'a* (Tea)__普陀茶__ -comes from the island of Pootoo which is one of the Chusan islands. Even though Pootoo is a small island it is very sacred to the Buddhist religion. From it comes Kuan Shi Yin, whose temple is located there.

This tea is beneficial in the treatment of hemorrhages such as haemoptysis or dysentery.

10. *Wu-i-Ch'a* (Tea)__武夷茶__ -is produced in the Wu-i Mountains. Located in the Fukien Province, the mountains are very beautiful with many cliffs; excellent tea is grown there. This is a dark tea which is used to release drunkenness, aid digestion and help stop dysentery.

11. *Chu-Lan-Ch'a* (Tea)__珠蘭__ -means pearl orchids. It is fragrant and very tasty to drink.

12. *Mo-Li Ch'a* (Tea)__茉莉__ -white jasmine, is packed with the tea in airtight boxes, as is Chu-Lan-Ch'a.

Chrysanthemum mixed with tea leaves—special chrysanthemum that is smaller is best when produced in Hang Chow Chekiang Province China, but now it is produced everywhere. Mixed with green teas, it can reduce fever, benefit the eyes and kidneys and detoxify.

White chrysanthemum should be dry and mulberry tree leaves, gathered in November, mixed together are especially good for the eyes and to reduce fever and flu.

A tea made of three pieces of ginger and three dates cooked with brown sugar can cure a cold and rheumatism.

Yeh-Ch'a, which means wild tea   野茶   and is grown among the cliffs, is regarded as the best tea by the Chinese.

CHAPTER 12:
THE RELATIONSHIP BETWEEN MAN AND WOMAN

Taoists believe that sex is like a chemical reaction that combines elements; man's sperm unites with woman's egg. They believe man and woman, yin and yang, can benefit each other. Yin and yang, like the chemical positive and negative, mix together to produce physical and mental effectiveness.

The famous Chinese Taoists and medical doctors, Tao-Hung Ching, of the fifth century A.D. and Sun Ssu-Mo of the seventh century, recognized the importance of sexuality for health. According to Taoist precepts, sex, far from hindering longevity, was beneficial to it. Fundamental to this principle was the idea of retaining as much as possible of the seminal essence and the divine element, primarily by causing the seminal fluid to return and nourish the brain. Formerly this technique was taught only to the emperor. Hwang Ti, the Yellow Emperor, had many wives and concubines; he practiced this technique and reigned for 100 years, until at last he became immortal. He recorded the discussions and experiments that he shared with his concubine Su Nu, and these are preserved in the form of the Su Nu Ching.[1]

There are two Taoist schools of thought on sex. One thinks sex can help achieve the goals of meditation, health,

longevity, and finally immortality. This school has had
many successful masters, such as Peng-Tzu, who, it is said,
lived 800 years.[2] Another is Master Li Ch'ing Yuen, who
lived through the eighteenth and ninteenth centuries and
the early part of the twentieth century, 250 years, marry-
ing fourteen times during his lifetime. The recently de-
ceased master, General Yang Sen, lived to be ninety-eight.
His obituary in the New York *Times* of May 17, 1977 attributes to him 43 children and over a score of wives and
concubines. One of the Nationalist Chinese magazines has
reported that at the time of his death General Yang Sen
had a twenty-one-year-old wife. History records many such
successes, not only restricted to the man but shared by man
and woman. In the Sung Dynasty, around the twelfth century A.D., there were seven enlightened masters. They
were called Ch'i Chen. Two of them, Ma Tan Yang and his
wife Sun Pu Erh Niang, meditated together, had three
sons, and at last reached immortality. Both received a title
from the emperor attesting to their spiritual achievements.

Li Ch'ing Yuen once replied to a student's question about
sex by saying the sperm in the body should be of a certain
quantity: If you are over the limit, it will flow out; if it is
lacking, you will be sick. When having sex, old sperm is
released and new sperm generated. This increases the
harmony of yin and yang and is highly beneficial for the
body.

The other school believes in extreme restraint with regard to sex. Sperm in the body is like gasoline in the car:
Without gasoline, the car does not move. Some masters
have reached high points in their mediation, but if they lose
their sperm, it is considered as if they had not done any
meditation at all. Such an attitude is seen in master Chiao
Pi Chen's book *Taoist Yoga: Alchemy and Immortality*,[3]
in which he responds to a question from an enlightened
seventy-year-old student on how to remedy his loss of the

positive principle (sperm) during the previous night's sleep; the master says he should begin his training all over again; only in this way might he regain the loss. But he warns the student to heed his advice, for, if he does not, he should go home and prepare to die.

The importance of retaining the vitality cannot be overestimated. Another student asks Chiao how to avoid nocturnal emissions; Chiao responds by teaching proper breathing and stressing the importance of the retention of the generative fluid in order that good health might endure. If the body is lacking in the generative fluid, he says, there is nothing to sustain it in the event of illness due to weather or unwholesome food. Untimely death can result.[4]

In Chapter 3 of the same book, he tells how to reproduce and sustain the generative force through *tan t'ien* breathing exercises.

1. Breathe in to drive the breath along the spinal column through the region of the coccyx up to the brain.

2. Breathe out to lower the breath from the throat to the abdomen and return it to the genital region.

3. Breathe in to raise it from the genital region to the lower abdomen and to the navel where the belt channel starts from both sides of the navel forming a belt (which circles the belly) and where the vital breath divides into two to reach the small of the back, then going up to both shoulders where it stops.

4. Breathe out to let it flow from both shoulders down into the outside of the arms to the outer sides of both wrists to the middle fingers before reaching the centers of both palms where it stops.

5. Breathe in to lift the breath from the centers of both palms into the inner sides of the arms up to the chest, where it stops.

6. Breathe out to drive the breath down to the belt channel where its two branches reunite below the navel before returning to the genital region.

7. Breathe in to lift it from the genital region into the region that extends from the groin up to two inches below the heart. On no account should it rise above the heart.

8. Breathe out to send it from under the heart down to the pubic region where it divides into two to descend in two channels on the outer sides of the legs and to the toes of the feet before reaching the centers of the soles of the feet where it stops.

9. Breathe in to raise it from the soles of the feet into the channels on the inner sides of the legs up to the pubic region and then to the lower abdomen where it stops.

10. Breathe out to send it from the lower abdomen to the genital region where it stops.

These ten breathing activities can clean every part of your body—arteries and veins, arms, legs, trunk, and head. They can clean the blood, stimulate the circulation, and dispel stagnation. Every organ can recover the condition it enjoyed when it was young.

Practice every day, in the morning after rising and in the evening before sleep, each time doing three to five cycles. In the beginning, the exercise might seem a little slow and unnatural, but after a few months, it will feel completely natural.

There are noteworthy parallels between the Taoist and Buddhist views of sex. In Buddhism there are also two schools: One absolutely restricts sex; the other, the Tantric school, is similar to the first school of Taoism, which considers sex beneficial to enlightenment. This school of Buddhism considers sex as an aid to meditation. The male organ, represented by lightning, is thought to be the yang. The female organ, represented by the lotus, is thought to be the yin. When united, they can achieve perfection. The essence of Buddha is thought to be in the female generative organ.

This school believes the mystical or divine energy of a

god (or of a Buddha) resides in his female counterpart, from which he received it in eternal embrace. The logical conclusion follows that the earthly yogi seeking perfection must also embrace his yogin in a sexual union *(maithuna)* prepared for with numerous rites and ceremonies. The monasteries of the Tantric school throughout Southeast Asia, Mongolia, and Tibet always have many statues and pictures depicting the Buddha in sexual union with a woman. This is called the Happy Buddha. The doctrine of the Tantric Yoga school includes the practice of sexual technique to help achieve the aim of meditation.

Confucius' view of sex is stated in his book *Doctrine of the Mean:*

> The way of the superior man may be found in its simple elements in the intercourse of common men and women; but here in its utmost reaches, it shines brightly through heaven and earth.[5]

And also in the same book, he states:

1. The way in which the superior man pursues reaches far and wide, and yet is secret.
2. Common men and women, however ignorant, may intermeddle with the knowledge of it; yet in its utmost reaches there is that which even the sage does not know. Common men and women, however much below the ordinary standard of character, can carry it into practice; yet in its utmost reaches there is that which even the sage is not able to carry into practice.[6]

The "utmost reaches" have to do with health, longevity, and the attainment of immortality.

Another facet of the Confucian school is stated by Mencius: "The desire of the child is towards his father and mother. When he becomes conscious of the attractions of beauty, his desire is towards young and beautiful women."[7]

One of Mencius' students, Kao Tze, is even more to the point. He maintains: To enjoy food and beauty, that is human nature.[8]

Finally, it is said there was once a hermit monk who adopted an orphan to be his disciple. They lived in the mountainous region for many years, isolated from society. Once he brought his disciple to the city, and the young monk was interested in the strange new environment. When he saw a young woman, he asked his master, "What is that?" The monk, not wanting the disciple to indulge in such thoughts, answered: "It's a tiger." When they returned to the monastery, the young monk pondered what he'd seen. His master asked, "What did you like most?" The young monk answered, "The tiger."

NOTES

1. Akira Ishihara and Howard S. Levy, trans. *The Tao of Sex* (New York: Harper and Row, 1968). See also Joseph Needham, *Science and Civilization in China*, vol. II (Cambridge: The University Press, 1954), p. 147.

2. See my *Taoist Health Exercise Book* (New York: Quick Fox, 1974), p. 135.

3. Translated by Lu K'uan Yu (New York: Samuel Weiser, 1973), chapter 10.

4. *Ibid.*

5. *The Chinese Classics*, James Legge, translator (Hong Kong: Hong Kong University Press, 1960), vol. I, p. 393.

6. *Ibid.*, pp. 391–92.

7. *Ibid.*, vol. II, p. 345.

8. *Ibid.*, p. 397.

CHAPTER 13:
PEACE OF MIND

In Chapter 2, we saw how the ancient Taoist and Confucian classics emphasized the importance of a peaceful mind for health, longevity, and the attainment of true wisdom. Study of the ancient classics is itself a helpful aid for the attainment of peace of mind, but it is much more important to put the practical advice they contain into effect in our daily lives. But how can this be done? It would seem that the fast pace and pressures of modern city life might make it difficult actually to live according to Taoist principles. But, though ancient China or rural Russia are places in which the peaceful attitude is more natural, this fact only serves to emphasize how much more the benefits of the Taoist attitude are needed in modern life, in which there are so many environmental dangers and threats to our health.

The most essential practical aspects of achieving peace of mind are quite simple. Don't insist on your ideas about how the world should be. Avoid thinking of events as "good" or "bad." Do not condemn or praise the fortunes or actions of others. Do not worry about your own personal loss or gain in dealing with others. Be happy with whatever comes to pass. If it appears that someone has done you harm, repay the injury with kindness. Do not be in a hurry to get anywhere or achieve anything. Don't concentrate or think too much or put too much energy into achieving your goals. Rest a lot.

Once you begin following this advice regularly in your life, it comes to seem very easy, and any initial difficulties seem trivial. It is a great comfort to be able to accept daily experience not in spite of its evils through the expectation of a heaven after death, but joyfully welcoming whatever it may bring us through an attitude that transcends the limitations of the distinction between good and evil. In this way we become happy through our harmony with the universe as a whole, and realize our heaven in the present.

Perhaps the greatest single insight in all this is that nothing in the world is either good or bad, right or wrong. Affairs simply appear to have value because of the limitation of one's point of view. Many Chinese stories and poems illustrate this insight in various ways. Among the most pleasing is to be found in the *Huai Nan Tzu*, by the Han dynasty writer Liu An.

According to the story, a farmer in Northern China, near the Mongolian border, discovered one day that his horse had disappeared. He knew not whether it had been lost or stolen and was put to great inconvenience, for he needed the horse for his work. His neighbors came to console him and grieved at the calamity that had befallen him. But the farmer would have none of it, pointing out that what had happened was not necessarily so bad, and so it did not warrant grief.

A few days later, the horse returned, accompanied by a magnificient Mongolian stallion that had strayed from its herd and followed along. This not only relieved the farmer's inconvenience but also greatly increased his wealth, for the horse was truly a prize. His friendly neighbors came rejoicing in his good fortune and envied him for the fine animal he had gotten through a stroke of luck. But the farmer did not rejoice with them, pointing out that what had happened was not necessarily so good.

Not long after that, the farmer's son was riding the Mongolian horse and found himself unable to control it, for his experience as a horseman was limited to riding the more docile plough horse. The frisky stallion threw him off, and his thigh was badly injured, leaving him lame. Although the farmer was again inconvenienced by this occurrence, he again refused to regard it as a misfortune, and did not grieve.

The next year the barbarian armies of the Mongolian chiefs swept into China, and every able-bodied young man was conscripted into the army to help defend the empire. The combat was heavy, and the mortality rate in the army was very high in many savage battles. But the farmer's son did not lose his life, for he was exempt from military service on account of his lame leg.

The farmer showed true wisdom, for his placid attitude was equally prepared for the possibility of good in what seemed evil and the possibility of evil in what seemed good. Thus he was able to remain equally happy throughout the whole course of events.